Listen to the Self-Doubt Voice: What do CYC Practitioners Experience?

Heather Sanrud

Listen to the Self-Doubt Voice: What do CYC Practitioners Experience?

LAP LAMBERT Academic Publishing

Impressum / Imprint
Bibliografische Information der Deutschen Nationalbibliothek: Die Deutsche
Nationalbibliothek verzeichnet diese Publikation in der Deutschen Nationalbibliografie;
detaillierte bibliografische Daten sind im Internet über http://dnb.d-nb.de abrufbar.
Alle in diesem Buch genannten Marken und Produktnamen unterliegen warenzeichen-,
marken- oder patentrechtlichem Schutz bzw. sind Warenzeichen oder eingetragene
Warenzeichen der jeweiligen Inhaber. Die Wiedergabe von Marken, Produktnamen,
Gebrauchsnamen, Handelsnamen, Warenbezeichnungen u.s.w. in diesem Werk berechtigt
auch ohne besondere Kennzeichnung nicht zu der Annahme, dass solche Namen im Sinne
der Warenzeichen- und Markenschutzgesetzgebung als frei zu betrachten wären und
daher von jedermann benutzt werden dürften.

Bibliographic information published by the Deutsche Nationalbibliothek: The Deutsche
Nationalbibliothek lists this publication in the Deutsche Nationalbibliografie; detailed
bibliographic data are available in the Internet at http://dnb.d-nb.de.
Any brand names and product names mentioned in this book are subject to trademark,
brand or patent protection and are trademarks or registered trademarks of their respective
holders. The use of brand names, product names, common names, trade names, product
descriptions etc. even without a particular marking in this works is in no way to be
construed to mean that such names may be regarded as unrestricted in respect of
trademark and brand protection legislation and could thus be used by anyone.

Coverbild / Cover image: www.ingimage.com

Verlag / Publisher:
LAP LAMBERT Academic Publishing
ist ein Imprint der / is a trademark of
OmniScriptum GmbH & Co. KG
Heinrich-Böcking-Str. 6-8, 66121 Saarbrücken, Deutschland / Germany
Email: info@lap-publishing.com

Herstellung: siehe letzte Seite /
Printed at: see last page
ISBN: 978-3-659-16148-3

Copyright © 2014 OmniScriptum GmbH & Co. KG
Alle Rechte vorbehalten. / All rights reserved. Saarbrücken 2014

TABLE OF CONTENTS

Table of Contents..1
List of Tables...4
List of Figures..5
Acknowledgements...6
Dedication..7
Quote..8
Chapter One – Introduction..9
The Inquiry of Self-Doubt in Child and Youth Care Practice............................9
Purpose of the Inquiry..10
Overview of the Inquiry..12
Chapter Two – A Literature Review...14
Burnout...15
The Imposter Phenomenon..17
Self-Efficacy..18
Self-Reflection...20
Self-Doubt...21
Summary...24
Chapter Three – Methodology – Design and Methods..............................27
Research Paradigm: A Phenomenological Approach....................................27
The Rationale for a Phenomenological Approach.......................................29
The Participants...30
The Process...33
The Interviews...38
Data Analysis..41
Summary..43
Validity..44

Issues related to Phenomenological Research..46
Chapter Four – Presentation of the Data..49
Stories of Self-Doubt..49
    Caroline's Story..49
    Marcie's Story..54
    Tracy's Story..58
    Penny's Story...62
Descriptions of Self-Doubt..67
    Caroline's Description...67
    Marcie's Description...75
    Tracy's Description...76
    Penny's Description..77
Themes of Self-Doubt..79
Discoveries and Impressions..81
    Essence of Self-Doubt...81
    Origins of Self-Doubt..82
    Categories of Self-Doubt..83
    Management of Self-Doubt..85
    Summary...87
Chapter Five – Finale..89
Implications for Child and Youth Care Practice...89
Further Research..90
Conclusion..92
References..94
Appendices..103
Appendix A – Flyer..104
Appendix B – Interview Questions..105

Appendix C – Photography of Art Release Form...106
Appendix D – Confidentiality Agreement for Typist/Transcriber..................107

List of Tables

Table 4.1

Central and Common Themes that Emerged from the Interview Data……………...80

List of Figures

Figure 4.1 Caroline's Drawing One……………………………………………….71

Figure 4.2 Caroline's Drawing Two……………………………………………….72

Figure 4.3 Caroline's Drawing Three……………………………………………...73

Figure 4.4 Caroline's Drawing Four……………………………………………….74

Acknowledgments

I am grateful for the support of my family and a special thank you goes to the following people for supporting and helping me see the process of this work through to the end . . .
Sibylle Artz for her spirited, consistent, and vital feedback,
Daniel Scott for his enlightening comments and questions,
Bruce Tobin for his tangible guidance and suggestions,
Martha Mattingly for adding that final critical remark which brought the inquiry to a close.

Finally, a heartfelt thank you to the four participants who embarked on the journey with me to explore and articulate their thoughts and feelings of self-doubt and to ponder the insights that emerged from the stories and descriptions.

Dedication

To the memory of my father

Harold W. Boyd

(1928 – 1985)

In his professional life my father instilled in me the importance of commitment and dedication. In his community life he demonstrated the qualities of nurturing and caring for others. In his academic life he exemplified the necessity of life-long learning. My father was always supportive of me and believed in my potential to achieve my dreams and aspirations. He would have been proud of what I have been able to accomplish.

Doubt camped out in the living room last week. I told him that we had had too many house guests. Doubt doesn't listen. He keeps saying the same thing again and again and again until I completely forget what I am trying to tell him. Doubt is demanding and not very generous, but I appreciate his honesty.

J. Ruth Gendler (1988, p. 21)

CHAPTER ONE
Introduction

Doubt is what gets you an education.

Wilson Mizner (Maisel, 1996)

The Inquiry into Self-Doubt in Child and Youth Care Practice

Listen. Listen. Listen to yourself. Listen to the self-doubt voice within. What is it telling you? Consider the following two vignettes of child and youth care practice.

Does this sound familiar? *Imagine you have just connected with a troubled teenage girl. You have spent 50 minutes with her, listening to her story, validating her feelings, and helping her define a few goals to effect change. You think the session went well and you are feeling confident that the relationship is forming nicely. The next appointment time arrives and the girl does not show up. What goes through your mind? Do you wonder if you could have done or said something differently? Do you expect too much of yourself? What do you feel in your body? Do you experience a sinking feeling in your "gut", as you wonder if you have done everything you could to ensure the girl's return? What do you feel emotionally? Do you wonder if you are really "cut out" for this kind of work? Do you begin to doubt your skills, knowledge, and ability to work effectively with teenagers?*

Or perhaps this sounds more familiar. *You enter a case conference meeting confidently. You are feeling on top of your practice and sit down comfortably in a chair. As the meeting progresses other people begin to talk about their cases and you become aware of feelings and thoughts of self-doubt creeping into your mind – " why can't I be that perceptive?" or " they seem more effective than I can ever be". You begin to doubt your own capabilities and are afraid to speak for fear of sounding stupid. Soon it is your turn to speak and you notice that your heart begins to beat more quickly and you can feel your hands getting sweaty. You shift uncomfortably in your chair and twist the top of your pen. Your voice hesitates slightly as you gather your thoughts about a family you have been working with in your practice. You wonder what you can learn from sharing your doubts and struggles with other colleagues?*

These paradigm examples suggest that self-doubt often occurs within an environment of uncertainty, anxiety, self-consciousness, illusions of self, insecurities, and ambiguity. Looking within and revealing these inner experiences of self-doubt may be risky, yet it can help professionals to remain in touch with their own perceptions and feelings about what they value and believe in their work. An understanding and exploration of self-doubt can lead to a growing awareness as professionals examine their inner thoughts, feelings, and bodily sensations in search of meaning and self-knowledge.

Purpose of the Inquiry

The purpose in researching this topic is to come to a more thorough understanding of the nature and meaning of self-doubt in child and youth care practice. The findings of this inquiry are useful for developing practitioner resiliency, enhancing the quality of supervision and education, and promoting a closer examination of self in practice. It contributes significant information to the child and youth care field about how practitioners value themselves, their profession, and their work. Also, discovering how others experience self-doubt is helpful. It is through the descriptions of others' experiences that much can be learned of our own. While listening to others' voices we may hear experiences similar to ours, gain more understanding, feel more confident, and feel less alone.

Pollio, Henley, and Thompson (1997) stress that people learn and relearn who they are on the basis of their encounters with others.

The study of self-doubt in practice is relevant to the professional and personal development of the practitioner. The findings from this inquiry will help practitioners and educators in the development of a greater degree of self-awareness and a more advanced capacity for reflective practice. Questioning motives and reasons for being, doing, and feeling can help practitioners become more authentic and ethical in their work. Gerson (1996) believes that when a place is provided for thoughtful clinicians to talk about the ways they think and work, amidst, and with their struggles, then an educational and enlightening experience is created. When practitioners become more reflective, and are able to articulate their thoughts and feelings more clearly, they can function in more meaningful and purposeful ways.

Learning how to address self-doubt in practice becomes an important aspect of practitioner self-awareness. Portnow (1996) believes "…that a fuller understanding of the phenomenon of mistrust of one's knowing has relevance for both clinicians and educators who share the singular experience of being companions to and participants in the growth and change of others" (p.4). Fewster (1990), Krueger (1997), and Ricks (1989), and others, discuss the importance of the self-awareness of the child and youth care practitioner to understand child and youth care work. Goldberg (1988), Ehrlich (2001), and Rousseve (1969) also suggest that the self-awareness of the counsellor is important to the vitality of the practitioner, is essential to understanding the therapeutic process, and is vital to sustaining professional and personal functioning.

Overview of the Inquiry

This inquiry evolved from my curiosity about self-doubt and my experiences and studies in child and youth care. It is a phenomenological inquiry into the lived experience of listening to, and understanding, the self-doubt voice of the child and youth care practitioner. The inquiry involved in-depth interviews with four child and youth care practitioners who have experienced self-doubt in their practice. I used a phenomenological approach to question how practitioners experience, live, and describe their self-doubt. This approach emphasizes the subjectivity of human experience and behavior and makes active participants of those who engage in the research process.

The goals of this inquiry are a) to come to a more thorough understanding of the meaning of self-doubt in practice, b) to understand the ways in which child and youth care practitioners experience self-doubt in their practice, and c) to provide a research-based grasp of the meaning and impact of self-doubt in child and youth care practitioners' practice, in order to inform child and youth care training and education. The questions that guided this inquiry are:

1. What do child and youth care practitioners experience when they experience self-doubt in their practice? What does it mean to them?
2. How do the practitioners describe their self-doubt in their practice? What does it look and feel like?
3. How does self-doubt affect their practice?
4. Are there different kinds of self-doubt in practice? What are they?
5. What can practitioners learn from their experiences of self-doubt?

The assumptions that influenced this inquiry developed from my own beliefs and experiences of self-doubt in professional practice. Practitioners are not alone with their thoughts and feelings about self-doubt. I believe that everyone, to some degree, experiences self-doubt in practice. Revealing these inner thoughts and feelings helps practitioners to identify who they are and what they do. It is relevant to their personal and professional growth. Understanding their thoughts and feelings of self-doubt enhances their ability to work to their fullest capacity. Thus, the intention of this inquiry was to better understand the lived experience of self-doubt in child and youth care practice.

Chapter One has introduced the inquiry, established its purpose, and provided an overview. Chapter Two discusses relevant literature related to self-doubt, and how this literature answers my research questions and identifies gaps. Chapter Three explains the research design, methods, and analysis I used to conduct a phenomenological inquiry. It also discusses research validity and issues related to phenomenological research. Chapter Four presents the data, noting stories, descriptions, themes, discoveries, and impressions of self-doubt in child and youth care practice. Chapter Five considers implications for child and youth care practice, suggestions for further research, and brings the inquiry to a close.

CHAPTER TWO
A Literature Review

I see that doubt has two faces,
one the heroic face of the eternal questioner,
the other the defeated face of the constant worrier.

Eric Maisel (1996)

A literature search on self-doubt in practice revealed little research on self-doubt in general, and none on the self-doubt of child and youth care practitioners. In fact, with respect to self-doubt, the personal voice and the subjective experience of the practitioner barely exist in the literature. Goldberg (1988) points out, "…in discussing the most human of sciences, authors have largely ignored an extremely significant component of this process – the practitioner" (p. 18). Abel & Nelson (1990) declare that " …few researchers have examined the expectations service workers bring to their jobs, so we know very little about their reactions to the obstacles they encounter" (p. 16). Goelman and Guo (1998) acknowledge there is a dearth of qualitative studies focusing on the experience of the practitioner. Hathaway (1999) notes "… few if any works have focused on self-doubt…" (p.3).

Hence, given the limited scope of literature describing self-doubt in practice, I decided to broaden my search. Other key words searched were burnout, uncertainty, self-evaluation, self-reflection, self-psychology, self-awareness, self-inquiry, self-consciousness, self-examination, self-efficacy, competence, anxiety, failure, criticism, insecurity, hesitation, the imposter phenomenon, and counsellor characteristics. The databases used were ERIC (Education Index), University of Victoria Catalogue, Web of Science, Psychinfo, Social Work Abstracts, Sociological Abstracts, Human and Social Sciences Index, and Dissertation Abstracts.

Because of this broadened search, the problem became one of selecting material which relates to my research questions, when no literature exists specifically relating to how child and youth care practitioners experience self-doubt. Therefore, while I read through the abstracts, generated from the search, the following topics emerged as somewhat relevant to my research questions: burnout, imposter phenomenon, self-efficacy, and self-reflection. The topic of burnout contained the most studies in the field of child and youth care. The literature on the imposter phenomenon sounded similar to self-doubt and the word self-doubt appeared in the literature on self-efficacy and self-reflection. As I read through the literature I began the process of sorting and selecting the specific studies that spoke directly to me about what child and youth care practitioners experience when they experience self-doubt in their practice.

Burnout

A substantial body of literature on burnout was found ranging from the 1970s to the late 1990s. Its relationship to self-doubt is apparent as often people who encounter thoughts and feelings of self-doubt in their practice also experience burnout. Freudenberger (1977) states burnout means, "…to fail, wear out, or become exhausted by making excessive demands on energy, strength, or resources" (p. 90). Goelman and Guo (1998) indicate that previous research (Freudenberger, 1977; Maslach & Pines, 1977; Mattingly, 1977; Boyd & Pasley, 1989; and Manlove 1993) has identified cynicism, negativism, and rigidity as common characteristics of burnout. Maslach (1982) was one of the first psychologists to study burnout in the early 1970s, and she makes a link between self-doubt and burnout, indicating that a person vulnerable to persistent feelings of self-doubt may be prone to burnout. She has helped to develop the "Maslach Burnout Inventory", which measures three aspects of the burnout phenomenon: emotional exhaustion, depersonalization, and reduced personal accomplishment. This inventory is used in both research studies and organizational programs.

I found eight studies (Freudenberger, 1977; Mattingly, 1977; McMullen & Krantz, 1988; Boyd & Pasley, 1989; Manlove, 1993; Savicki, 1993; Lambert, 1994; Goelman & Guo, 1998), which focused on burnout in the field of child and youth care. Mattingly paints a poignant picture of child and youth care workers and their growing doubts about their clinical practice. She writes that it is essential for the worker to "…tolerate ambiguity…" (p. 130) and to continue "…to reestablish for himself (sic) his sense of 'Who am I?' and 'What do I do?' " (p. 131). She notes that when feelings of doubts and inadequacies are shared they are often met with denial and an unsympathetic ear. Mattingly concludes that with more support from, and trust in colleagues, there is more opportunity for reflection on one's practice. She confirms that "[t]he emerging associations of child care workers also have an important role in helping workers with the problems of stress and burn-out" (p. 136).

Lambert (1994) suggests that burnout is a process and begins with feelings of self-doubt. She discusses taking a "multi-dimensional" approach to identifying causes of burnout, constructive ways of overcoming it, and effective ways of observing how burnout is manifested in child care settings. Freudenberger (1977) notes childcare workers can protect themselves against burnout when they have personal insights often and when they share doubts as well as successes in an honest and open fashion. He concludes:

> Not seeing our own loneliness, deprivation, or personality flaws is a tragic form of pride and unconscious narcissism. It is tragic because it hurts the youth and it deprives us of the pleasure of seeing a little bit better who we are at this point in our lives, why we work and do what we do, and what we could become if we were more authentic. (p. 98)

McMullen and Krantz (1988) studied burnout in 67 day-care workers and were particularly interested in the association between self-esteem, learned helplessness, and burnout. Their study found that emotional exhaustion and depersonalization were significantly related to learned helplessness. Boyd and Pasley (1989) and Manlove (1993) found that role ambiguity is a strong predictor of burnout. Savicki (1993) examined the connection between the social climate of the work environment and burnout. He noted, since burnout and job stress "continue to plague the field" (p. 441), that the identity of child and youth care practitioners is a vital concern and that there is concern for the health of the profession, particularly of its members (the practitioners).

Finally, Maslach (1982) notes people who are tuned into their inner feelings, who are introspective, and who understand themselves well, are better able to cope with, and overcome burnout. Similarly, Pines and Aronson (1998) found when nurses did not share their innermost feelings, their levels of stress increased, resulting in feelings of inadequacy in their practice. Therefore, it would seem that sharing feelings of self-doubt with others helps practitioners recognize that they are not alone. This also supports the notion of the importance of practitioner self-awareness and self-reflection and the ability to share insights with others.

The Imposter Phenomenon

Another close link to self-doubt is found in the literature on the imposter phenomenon. Clance and Imes (1978) developed the term imposter phenomenon to designate "an internal experience of intellectual phoniness". Clance and Imes (1978), Clance (1985), Clance and O'Toole (1987), and Langford and Clance (1993) acknowledge this internal experience included feelings of uncertainty about performance, feelings of anxiety, an unrealistic sense of self-competency, a fear of failure, and an inability to internalize strengths and accept deficits. Clance and

Imes and Clance and O'Toole discovered self-doubt plays a strong role in some women's lives who experience the imposter phenomenon. Clance (1985) developed an "Imposter Phenomenon Scale" to measure the presence of imposter feelings. Clance (1985) and Langford and Clance (1993) noted a link between childhood experiences and the feelings of the imposter phenomenon in adulthood.

Allen (1997) studied first and second year graduate students and school counsellors already working in the field. She used Clance's Imposter Phenomenon Scale and found that 9 out of the 48 respondents had feelings of the Imposter Phenomenon (IP). She states, "This suggests that as a profession, counsellors and counsellors-in-training do experience the IP to a significant degree" (p. 41). Allen believes in the importance of counsellors being able to communicate personal values and establishing a firm sense of self. Allen concludes that counsellors who experience imposter feelings "... may have difficulties utilizing and working to the fullest of their capabilities, because of the negative feelings associated with the IP. The counselling field can readily recognize the great potential that may be lost" (p. 48).

Self-efficacy

Since doubt can surface when individuals lose confidence in their abilities to perform certain tasks, I selected five studies which discussed self-efficacy. Bandura and Adams (1977) and Bandura (1980, 1989, 1997) researched self-efficacy and defined self-efficacy as the belief that one's ability to perform a certain task is based on personal experience, spoken personal beliefs, and physiological state. Bandura (1997) speculates that people with high self-efficacy believe that they can achieve what they set out to do and as a result they are healthier, more effective, and generally more successful than those with low self-efficacy expectations. Bandura (1989) noted those with low self-efficacy are plagued with more self-doubts:

> Self-doubts can set in quickly after some failures or reverses. The important matter is not that difficulties arouse self-doubt, which is a natural immediate reaction, but the speed of recovery of perceived self-efficacy from difficulties. Some people quickly recover their self-assurance; others lose faith in their capabilities. Because the acquisition of knowledge and competencies usually requires sustained effort in the face of difficulties and setbacks, it is resiliency of self-belief that counts. (p.1176)

Wimett (1992) found that "[e]fficacy beliefs can influence performance" (p. 11). She researched self-efficacy in registered nurses and found that nurses gained more confidence in their nursing abilities from a positive role model. The responses to a survey which asked what undermined the nurses' belief in their nursing abilities, were divided into the following four categories:

1. lack of education, knowledge, experience
2. other people and self
3. the system (lack of support and supervision)
4. time (pressures and not enough)

Pelham (1991) found " . . . that people possess both epistemic and emotive investments in their self-views" (p. 527). What people think, feel, and know about themselves influence who they are, what they do, and how they do it, thus showing a strong connection between self-efficacy, confidence, and the absence or presence of self-doubt.

Elks and Kirkhart (1993) conducted a qualitative study to develop a deeper understanding of how social work practitioners evaluate themselves in their practice. They found that the practitioners acknowledged difficulty in really knowing their own effectiveness. Elks and Kirkhart assert, " . . . the presence of doubts about knowing one's effectiveness appears to be more a philosophical concern than one that directly impinges on practice" (p. 556). If this is the case, then how *does* self-doubt affect practice?

Self-reflection

Self-reflection and self-awareness (introspection) are critical to the understanding of self and of others (Eckroth-Bucler, 2001; Fewster, 1990; Goldberg, 1993; Kreuger, 1997; Lauterback & Becker, 1996; Ricks, 1989). Self-reflection can help practitioners explore their self-doubt in practice. Schön (1983) and Mezirow (1990) have both contributed much to the field of self-reflection. Schön identifies a " . . . process of reflection-in-action which is central to the "art" by which practitioners sometimes deal well with situations of uncertainty, instability, uniqueness, and value conflict" (p. 50). This can be an important action for day-to-day and continuous improvement of competency in practice. Mezirow demonstrates how reflection can enable practitioners to critique the presuppositions on which their beliefs have been built. Through reflection practitioners can change distortions in their beliefs and make meaning from this process. Mezirow points out, "[t]o make meaning means to make sense of an experience; we make an interpretation of it. When we subsequently use this interpretation to guide decision making or action, then making meaning becomes learning" (p. 1).

Self-reflection could be an educational and valuable tool for deepening the meaning and understanding of self-doubt. Activities designed to encourage self-reflection on the topic of self-doubt in practice could help practitioners develop more professionally and personally. However, Brookfield (1994) found that critical reflection led to self-doubt, feelings of isolation, and uncertainty in a group of adult graduate students who participated in activities designed to promote critical reflection. This leads me to wonder if this would be the case if the participants *knowingly* and *purposefully* were reflecting critically on their own feelings of self-doubt. What would self-reflection reveal to them then?

Self-doubt

Only six studies emerged from the literature search, which speak directly to the topic of self-doubt. Bendixen (2002) explored the phenomenology of epistemic doubt, which she describes as the continuous questioning of the existence and possibility of absolute knowledge. Her study focused on how adults perceive and describe their own epistemic doubt and how they have resolved this doubt. She discovered when people doubt their own knowledge this impacts their experience and resolution of self-doubt. Bendixen identified four components of doubt: the triggers of epistemic doubt, the experience of epistemic doubt, the resolution of epistemic doubt, and the results of the doubting process. She was specifically interested in the role epistemic doubt plays in epistemological development and change. She found that reflection and social interaction motivated participants to change their epistemological beliefs. One of the participants in Bendixen's study stated without the pain of doubt there is no growth (change).

Hermann, Leonardelli, and Arkin (2002) link self-doubt with self-esteem. They conducted three studies. In two of the studies, they found people high in self-doubt feel more threatened when asked to retrieve past experiences of self-confidence than those with low self-doubt. The self-esteem of people high in self-doubt decreased as well. The third study " . . . was designed to investigate the phenomenology associated with low self-doubt" (p. 404). The findings of this study suggest that people low in self-doubt may be better at deflecting threats when they possess more positive feeling of self-worth. A self-doubt subscale (Oleson, Poehlmann, Yost, Lynch & Arkin, 2000) was used in the first and second study as part of data gathering, and in the third to prescreen participants. Oleson et al.

(2000) developed a 17-item Subjective Overachievement Scale, which includes two subscales measuring individual differences in self-doubt and concern with performance. Although this tool may be useful for investigating self-doubt, Herman et al. and Oleson et al. are more concerned with measuring the presence of self-doubt broadly, not with wanting to deepen an understanding of what people experience when they encounter self-doubt.

Hathaway (1999) explored the experience of self-doubt as a " … thematic exploration of the multifaceted phenomenon of self-doubt, looking at intrapsychic structures and realities, intrapersonal realities, and collective and mythic cultural realities, all of which profoundly impact, and are impacted by, the experience of self" (p. 4). Hathaway worked with the concepts of feeling and thinking, and myth, and grappled with defining, describing, and understanding self-doubt. She investigated the theories of Carl Jung, James Hillman, Sylvan S. Tomkins, Wilfred Bion, and D.W. Winnicott, as well as three myths, to help her analyze a written "phenomenological statement" of images of self-doubt in a woman's life. Hathaway concludes "self-doubt is a crisis in being" (p. 294), meaning a person is alienated from her self, her family, her relationship with others, and her culture. She found, " [i]t is a crisis in which there is a fluctuation and a conflict in thought and feeling which gives rise to a disorientation about what is real, what is possible, what is good." (p. 294).

Portnow's (1996) study explored the ways that eight adult men and eight adult women describe their experiences of self-doubt and mistrust of knowing. She defines mistrust of knowing "…as individuals' disbelief in or dismissal of the validity of their feelings, needs or interpretations of experience" (p. 3). Her study reveals two kinds of self-doubt, "developmental doubt" and "dispositional doubt". Simply, developmental doubt involves the loss of confidence while still retaining a sense that one can learn and know, and dispositional doubt involves a loss of confidence in oneself as a knower. She found that a person's relationship to his/her knowing plays an important role in the way he/she will experience and interpret challenges to, and supports for his/her needs, feelings, and sense-making. While Hathaway and Portnow's studies have produced some thought-provoking findings in everyday life, I wonder how people experience self-doubt in their professional life.

Abrams and Kessler (2002) explored the "... doubts, angst, self-inquiry, and inner struggles ... " (p. 6) of counsellors from a narrative perspective. They provide no further analysis other than suggesting, as Resta (2002) claims, "... each vignette offers an opportunity for personal and professional growth and evolution" (p. 23). Listening to similar stories helps practitioners realize they are not alone and that growth and change can come from giving voice to their self-doubts. Bendixen (2000) refers to this in her study as well.

Finally, Hiebert, Uhlemann, Marshall, and Lee (1998) examined "... the self-talk pattern of counsellor-trainees to determine how self-talk relates to anxiety level and the performance of counselling skills in a prepracticum setting" (p. 164). They hypothesized that there would be a close link between counsellor self-talk and anxiety level and that these variables would affect counsellor performance. They suggest:

> ... higher levels of anxiety are associated with higher levels of negative self-talk and lower levels of positive self-talk. Higher levels of anxiety are also associated with lower levels of performance on a video-taped counselling interview. Moreover, decreases in negative self-talk are associated with decreases in anxiety, increases in positive self-talk, and better performance on a video-taped counselling interview. (p. 168)

Summary

In this review, I have explored how several topics relevant to self-doubt have been treated in the literature. The empirical explorations of burnout, the imposter phenomenon, self-efficacy, and self-reflection suggest some interesting implications for understanding self-doubt.

The literature on burnout has established that feelings of self-doubt contribute to burnout in one's profession. The studies also purport that professional helpers need to share personal insights and feelings of doubt often to fully understand the ambiguity of their role and identity in the helping and caring professions.

The literature on the imposter phenomenon shows that people who experience self-doubt also experience feelings of the imposter phenomenon. It also suggests it is important for counsellors to know themselves well so that they may work to their fullest capacity.

Similarly, the literature on self-efficacy links self-doubt with performance. When people believe in their capabilities they have more confidence and are more resilient in their work. People who experience the imposter phenomenon are not aware of their own effectiveness and doubt their capabilities, as the literature on self-efficacy has affirmed. Yet, what do practitioners experience when they doubt their own effectiveness in their practice? What does it mean to them when they doubt their own effectiveness? What self-awareness do they gain from this experience?

What this literature does not answer is how practitioners describe their self-doubt, explain what it means to them, and what they can learn from their experiences. The literature provides some hints, suggestions, and clues about how burnout, the imposter phenomenon, and self-efficacy affect practice, yet it lacks *specific* details, explanations, and descriptions about how it affects practice.

Furthermore, the literature on self-reflection claims it is critical for professionals to reflect on who they are and what they bring to their work. This helps them to understand more fully the meaning of what they do, of the self-doubt they experience, and of how they can work to the best of their ability. Reflecting on one's self-doubt in practice helps professionals to gain more insight into what they believe and value about their practice and this contributes to more learning. Specific examples of what child and youth care professionals experience in their work are missing in this literature.

Finally, the literature on self-doubt itself describes how self-doubt is manifested in everyday life. People do not trust what they know and when they have low self-esteem they doubt themselves more and feel more threatened. The literature also notes how the inner dialogue of counsellors contributes to experiences of doubt and anxiety in practice. It is interesting to note the relationship between anxiety and self-talk and its impact on counsellor performance. I wonder if there is such a relationship between self-doubt and self-talk, and how this would affect a child and youth care practitioner's performance.

The profession of child and youth care is very demanding work. It takes a confident and resilient professional to immerse herself in the lives of the many children, youth, and families she serves to try to understand the challenges they face and discover creative ways of helping them to deal with or overcome these challenges. Caring intimately about others while maintaining professional and personal boundaries involves great integrity and competency in interpersonal skills. It is also vital for child and youth care professionals to possess self-awareness so that they may look within to discover how they are impacted by the work. It is through this process of self-reflection that practitioners can learn from their experiences of self-doubt in their practice and discover what child and youth care work means to them.

Much of the literature I have selected for this review has come from other professions including nursing, social work, and counselling. While a rich and provocative literature does exist in the field of child and youth care none could be found which speaks directly to the experience of self-doubt in child and youth care practice.

One of the major gaps in the literature is that while a few professions have been studied with respect to the topic of self-doubt, child and youth care has not. There is no written evidence that the field knows what child and youth care professionals experience when they face self-doubt in their practice. Moreover, given the field's emphasis on self-awareness (Fewster, 1990; Kreuger, 1997; Ricks, 1989) it is surprising that there is very little written on the self-doubt of the child and youth care professional. Therefore, this inquiry into self-doubt is necessary for the further development of the education and field of child and youth care.

CHAPTER THREE
Methodology – Design and Methods

Phenomenology is used to obtain knowledge about how we think and feel in the most direct ways. Its focus is what goes on within the person in an attempt to get to and describe lived experience in a language as free from the constructs of the intellect and society as possible. At its root, the intent is to understand phenomena in their own terms – to provide a description of human experience as it is experienced by the person herself.

Bentz and Shapiro (1998, p. 96)

Research Paradigm: A Phenomenological Approach

A qualitative approach is suitable for describing human experiences in uniquely human ways and often invites participants to join the researcher in making sense of the experiences that are being investigated. Pollio, Henley, and Thompson (1997), van Manen (1997), and Giorgi (1985) state that the world of human beings is meant to be lived and described. Qualitative researchers are interested in studying human experiences from a scientific perspective that is field focused, participant centered, and process oriented. Creswell (1998) states:

> Qualitative research is an inquiry process of understanding based on distinct methodological traditions of inquiry that explore a social or human problem. The researcher builds a complex, holistic picture, analyzes words, reports detailed views of informants, and conducts the study in a natural setting. (p. 15)

Thus, to study child and youth care practitioners' experiences of their self-doubt in practice means to explore a human phenomenon in its natural environment. Within the range of qualitative approaches available I chose a phenomenological method of interviewing described by Kvale (1996) and Seidman

(1991) and an analysis based on Hycner's (1985) guidelines for the phenomenological analysis of interview data. As a qualitative researcher, I joined each participant in the interviews and entered her world to generate the data which came in the form of words, stories, metaphors, and drawings. During the interviews, I sought the participants' descriptions, meanings, and understandings of the phenomenon of self-doubt. Boeree (1998) suggests that such an approach allows the phenomenon to reveal itself in all its fullness. In my interviews, participants discussed self-doubt, described it, and reflected upon the meaning of their experiences in their own words and images. In the process, the participants and I were able to come to a deeper and fuller understanding of what they experience when they experience self-doubt in their daily practice.

Phenomenological inquiry involves listening to, watching, conversing with, and engaging in empathic understanding of another person (Bentz & Shapiro, 1998; Kvale, 1996). This invites a human interaction and Kvale notes it is within this interaction that "knowledge evolves" (p. 125). Bentz and Shapiro (1998) acknowledge phenomenological inquiry is an experiential approach where the researcher allows the data to come forward in the interviews by losing herself in the pacing and the language of the other. This creates an atmosphere for empathic understanding. This means the researcher fully participates in the personal and face-to-face structure of the interview seeking to understand what is being described. Janesick (1994) states, "This means the researcher must have the ability to observe behavior and must sharpen the skills necessary for observation and face-to-face interview" (p. 212). As I have much professional training and experience in education, counselling, and child and youth care and have struggled with my own feelings, thoughts, and behaviors of self-doubt, I was comfortable with immersing myself completely in the interviews and giving my full attention to what each participant said.

This type of methodology encourages a deeper understanding of the meaning of lived experience (van Manen, 1997). Therefore, choosing the transcendental (descriptive) tradition of phenomenology (Moustakas, 1994) as a conceptual framework helped me to focus on description and delve deeply into the meaning and understanding of self-doubt as the participants described their experiences openly during the interviews. Moustakas states that "...transcendental phenomenology is a scientific study of the appearance . . . of phenomena just as we see them and as they appear to us in consciousness" (p.49), and this leads ". . . to knowledge in an absolute sense . . . knowledge that emerges from a transcendental or pure ego, a person who is open to see what is, as it is, and to explicate what is in its own terms" (pp. 40-41). Sokolowski (2000) describes the transcendental ego as that part of the human being that is representative of reason and truth. Thus, during the interviews the participants spoke freely and truthfully from their own experience and described self-doubt as they saw it, felt it, and thought about it from their own consciousness. The phenomenological method of interviewing created a process of generating data from the spoken word and drawn image of self-doubt, through which awareness, understanding, and knowledge were derived.

Kvale (1996), Seidman (1991), Hycner (1985), and Moustakas (1994) have provided me with the theoretical framework that has informed the design of my study. These four authors assisted me in defining what it was I wanted to do and how I was going to do it. Since phenomenology is so vast, both as a philosophy and as a research method, I found selecting authors with whom I could resonate helped me to shape my thinking and approach to this study.

The Rationale for a Phenomenological Approach

A phenomenological method is well suited to address the research question of what it is that child and youth care practitioners experience when they experience self-doubt in practice, because my intention is to listen, illuminate, and understand another person's experience. Thus, phenomenological inquiry is a method which illuminates a phenomenon and helps us to understand it. This inquiry has allowed me to explore data in the form of individual stories, images, and descriptions of self-doubt for the purpose of understanding the meaning of what each practitioner experiences in her practice. I was able to come to a richer and deeper understanding of the context in which the participants find meaning in what they think, feel, and do about the self-doubt in their practice. Ultimately, the participants experienced this understanding as well, as they told me so during the interviews. One participant stated, "Oh, just the fact of drawing it and talking about it (self-doubt) and then having a greater understanding". Another participant stated she continued to think about her self-doubt after the first interview was over.

Further, a phenomenological approach is appropriate for this inquiry as it allowed the lived experience of self-doubt to be illuminated naturally without a formal scientific hypothesis formulated by me, the researcher. Hycner (1985) confirms that the phenomenological researcher "… wants to be as open to the phenomenon as possible without constricting his/her perspective by placing the phenomenon on the promethian bed of hypothesis testing" (p.299). Further, Moustakas (1994) states:

> Phenomenology is the *first* method of knowledge because it begins with "things themselves"; it is also the final court of appeal. Phenomenology, step by step, attempts to eliminate everything that represents a prejudgment, setting aside presuppositions, and reaching a transcendental state of freshness and openness, a readiness to see in an unfettered way, not threatened by the customs, beliefs, and prejudices of normal science, by the habits of the natural world or by knowledge based on unreflected everyday experience. (p.41)

To the best of my ability, I maintained a phenomenological attitude of faithfulness to the phenomenon of self-doubt throughout the inquiry by putting my beliefs and assumptions aside "into brackets" or "into parentheses" (Sokolowski, 2000). This means I listened attentively and remained open to each participant as she described her worldview of self-doubt and set my presuppositions aside as much as possible by bracketing them (suspending my judgments). This concept of reaching an ideal neutral position without any previous understanding on my part is difficult and as Pollio, Henley, and Thompson (1997) recognize, assuming an opposing explanation that complete bracketing is impossible to achieve ". . . ignores the contextualized nature of human understanding ... (p.46). I came to this inquiry with some understanding of the phenomenon and as Pollio et al claim "[t]o avoid conceptual inadequacy, a positive application of bracketing is needed, one that does not assume or require neutrality as an ideal or even an attainable perspective (p.47). Therefore, the process of writing in a journal helped me to be more attuned to my presuppositions and prior understandings and bracket them more realistically. This is explained more fully in the Process Section.

The Participants

Hycner (1985) points out "[d]oing this kind of phenomenological research ... requires that only a limited number of people be interviewed given the vast amount of data that emerges from one interview" (p. 295). With this in mind I set a goal to interview four candidates who were willing to volunteer their time and could fully describe their experiences of self-doubt. Choosing four participants seemed reasonable as I approached four human service organizations that represented a range of sites that employ child and youth care practitioners in one community.

I used a purposive sampling strategy (Neuman, 2004) to select participants for this inquiry. The purpose was to find suitable candidates who were child and youth care practitioners, were knowledgeable about self-doubt, have experienced self-doubt in their practice, were willing to talk about it, and shared my interest in wanting to make meaning of this experience (Gall, Borg & Gall, 1996). With these criteria in mind I created a flyer (Appendix A) and approached four human service organizations, that employ child and youth care practitioners, and made an appointment to visit during a team meeting to introduce myself and explain my study. Copies of the flyer were handed out to child and youth care practitioners to allow them to make their own choices to participate and contact me directly by a specific date, August 31, 2003. This also ensured the anonymity of the involvement of the participants. Seidman (1991) suggests, "[t]he more care and thoroughness interviewers put into making contact, the better foundation they establish for the interviewing relationship" (p. 37).

Four people expressed interest in participating and contacted me. After briefly connecting with each participant to ask if she indeed fit the criteria, I gathered contact information and scheduled the first interview. I informed the participants about the nature and purpose of the research and what their participation would involve, including any possible risks or benefits as noted in an informed consent of which each participant received a copy. Also, as the participants have the right to privacy, I was mindful of maintaining anonymity and confidentiality, and therefore chose the following pseudonyms for each participant: Caroline, Marcie, Tracy, and Penny.

Further, throughout this inquiry I use the pronouns "she" and "her" as all participants who came forward were females. I considered extending the date on the flyer into the fall of 2003 to see if any male child and youth care practitioners were interested in participating, but decided that I needed to move my inquiry along as my time was quickly running out. This was one of those unpredictable decisions Janesick (1994) indicates that takes place in the field. Moreover, I am a female researcher and this may have accounted for women being willing to volunteer for my study. There may be a sense of safety women feel when they are with other women. I was also aware that the community organizations I visited employ a majority of female workers. In fact, at one agency only women were present during one of the team meetings I attended.

Further, it is important to amplify the voice of women in the field of child and youth care as Parry (1989, 1992) and Sladde (2001) comment on the role and influence of women in child and youth care and the importance of raising the visibility of women in the field. Parry (1992) notes that there are gender differences and woman have the potential to be influential. Ricks (1992) speaks about a feminist perspective to caring in child and youth care. Belenky, Clinchy, Goldberger, and Tarute (1986) have extensively explored how women experience themselves as learners and knowers. While it is not my intent to debate gender here, I recognize it presents a limitation to my study. It would be interesting to hear from men about what they experience when they experience self-doubt in their practice and discover what the gender differences are. Perhaps self-doubt in care professions has gender implications. Further research is definitely warranted in this area.

The Process

Based on Kvale's (1996) work I conducted conversational in-depth interviews with four female child and youth care practitioners about their experiences of self-doubt in their practice. He notes ". . . *an interview whose purpose is to obtain descriptions of the life world of the interviewee with respect to interpreting the meaning of the described phenomena*" (p.p. 5-6, italics in the original) is a research method that has structure and purpose. The purpose of my interviews was to hear and understand the participants' descriptions about their experiences of self-doubt and to make meaning from these descriptions. The structure of the interview included questions (see Appendix B) that encouraged a story to be told. People describe their experiences best by telling stories. Seidman (1991) supports storytelling in research as a way of knowing and understanding. He says, "[t]elling stories is essentially a meaning-making process" (p. 1), and reflection and meaning-making evolved throughout the interviews. This approach supported the process of individuals making meaning of their own experiences of self-doubt through a personal method of interviewing and storytelling in an interactive, interpersonal, and person-centered context. Pollio, Henley, and Thompson (1997) state that "[w]ithin the context of phenomenological interviewing, questions have a descriptive and facilitative purpose rather than one of assessing a preexisting opinion, attitude, or level of knowledge" (p. 35).

The interviews were like conversations as I listened actively and responded to the participants' descriptions using empathic responses to communicate understanding, and open-ended questions to elicit personal stories and in-depth descriptions and to move the interviews along. A relationship developed quickly between the interviewees and myself as I used respect, genuineness, and sensitivity to create an open, personable, and collaborative atmosphere. I approached each interview with the willingness to hear and understand what the participants were saying about their self-doubt so that I could decipher meaning.

To invite the process of making art during the interviews I simply stated that I was a child and youth care practitioner trained in art therapy and if the participants wanted to create a picture of what they were talking about in the interviews they were welcome to do so. As I was not asked, I did not talk extensively about my art therapist title, nor did I give elaborate detail about what an art therapist does. This information may have intimidated the participants and I wanted to create an informal, non-expert, and person-centered approach (Carl Rogers, 1961) to the interviews. I also wanted to listen intently to the experiences of each participant and not influence what they would say or do during the interview process. Thus, I simply invited each participant to create a picture of self-doubt if she chose to do so.

This was not a forced activity. The choice was completely up to each participant and the art materials (paper, felt markers, pastels, cut out pictures from magazines, scissors, and glue) were readily available to her as they were placed in a wicker basket within arm's reach. This person-centered approach (Rogers, 1961) is important as it speaks to my belief that the participants are the experts on their own experience and are capable of making their own decisions. This act needed to be strictly voluntary and it evidently was, as only one participant out of the four created art. For example, during the second interview Caroline selected paper and pastels and drew her experience of self-doubt while she was clarifying her words from the first interview (this is described more fully in the Interview Section). This art then became data, along with the recorded stories and descriptions. To include the art and present it as data I took photographs of these drawings, with Caroline's permission (see Appendix C for the photography release and consent form).

During the interviews the stories took shape in the form of words and visual art. Seidman (1991) states that, "[a]t the very heart of what it means to be human is the ability of people to symbolize their experience through language" (p. 2) and McNiff (1996) would argue through art as well. As a trained art therapist I was comfortable facilitating an art making process during an interview because I am familiar with how people can gain insight from making art. Also, because of my art therapy training I was able to ask open-ended questions during the act of making art that would not take away from the interview process. Some of these questions included: What do these colours represent? Tell me more about what the lines mean in this drawing. What does this shape represent and mean for you? The drawings visually could show what the participants were saying verbally about self-doubt. Also, participants were able to draw and talk at the same time and this created an auditory record of words as well as a visual one.

I informed the participants that photographs and negatives of the art images, transcripts, analysis notes, computer discs, original art images, and audiotapes would all be locked in a filing cabinet until the completion of the inquiry. Within six months of completion of this text remaining photographs and negatives of the art images, transcripts, analysis notes, computer discs, and audiotapes will be destroyed. Original art images will be returned to the participant. Consent forms will be kept in a locked filing cabinet for one year after at which time they will be destroyed.

Further, I scheduled interviews that would be convenient for each participant. Since I began the interview process in September of 2003 and completed it in April of 2004, attention was also given to the management of my time due to the length of the study. I adjusted my schedule accordingly and remained flexible to the participants' needs, as well as to my own. Janesick (1994) points out that "... decisions made during the study usually concern effective use of time, participants' issues, and researcher issues [b]ecause working in the field is unpredictable a good deal of the time . . . " (p. 213).

I also gave special consideration to choosing a location for the interviews. Accessibility, privacy, and solitude helped to determine the suitability for the interviewing space. After a brief consultation with each participant it was decided that the interviews would take place in a private office or in the participant's home. Participants chose which setting would work best for them at the time of each interview.

Moreover, to maintain an unprejudiced presence and phenomenological attitude during the interviews and to help me bracket my own personal experiences and biases of self-doubt, I kept a journal and recorded my thoughts, feelings, and images as they unfolded for me during the course of the inquiry. Bracketing is an important exercise in phenomenological research and Denzin (1989) explains that a researcher must put her self aside, so that the phenomenon can be experienced as it is. Ely, Vinz, Downing, and Anzul (1997) note that researchers must distance themselves from the phenomenon under study in order to remain objective.

Bracketing is a difficult task, yet to the best of my ability I "put my self aside" and distanced myself from the phenomenon as I noted my own personal observations, reflections, experiences, metaphors, art images, and musings about my theories, assumptions, and experiences of self-doubt in a personal journal. Meloy (1994) notes that the personal journal can become a resource of the researcher's own creation and experience. Therefore, this became an important process for me because I grapple with much self-doubt myself, and as Creswell (1998) points out the phenomenological researcher must bracket " . . . preconceptions so as not to inject hypotheses, questions, or personal experiences into the study" (p. 33). Kvale (1996) also indicates that the researcher must critically analyze these presuppositions as well. Thus, my own writing and art making process helped me to explore my inner world separate from the participants', allowing me to remain open and present to their world during the interviews and analysis of the data. This also led me to an empathic understanding of what self-doubt means to each participant because empathy involves "…the feeling, or the thinking, of one personality into another until some state of identification is achieved. In this identification real understanding between people can take place…" (May, 1989, p.63).

The Interviews

I structured one 120-minute (two hour) conversational in-depth interview, one 60-minute (one hour) interview to validate each participant's description for accuracy, and one 30-minute follow-up session to share the results and to thank each participant for her involvement. The 120-minute and 60-minute interviews were both audio taped with the participants full agreement. The 30-minute follow-up session was not audio taped. Since this inquiry involved human participants, people were informed of all details of participation by means of an informed consent. Before the start of the in-depth (first) interview I explained the entire process and each participant read and signed the informed consent. Participants received a copy of this consent to keep for their own records. I also invited each participant to ask questions throughout the entire process and I reminded her that her participation was completely voluntary and that she could withdraw at any time.

During the interview I asked each participant the same set of questions (Appendix B). Other questions also emerged, which helped the participants to describe their experiences more fully. Seidman (1991) states, "[t]he goal is to have the participant reconstruct his or her experience within the topic under study" (p. 9). Such open-ended questions helped me to listen more closely to what the speaker was saying: "Can you tell me more about…? What was your experience of that when …? Could you describe in detail what you mean when you say . . . ? (Kvale, 1996, pp. 133-135). These questions helped the participants to build upon and explore their responses more deeply. Kvale further suggests "[t]here is the phenomenological ideal of listening … allowing the interviewees' descriptions of their experiences [to] unfold without interruptions from interviewer questions and the presuppositions these involve" (p. 135). Thus, I became very mindful about my role as an interviewer during this first interview.

Once each 120-minute interview was completed it was transcribed. To manage the amount of typing this generated I asked an experienced typist to help me transcribe the interviews. I also asked the typist to help me type the stories, descriptions, and summaries of the interviews and portions of this text. To protect the anonymity of the participants this typist signed a confidentiality agreement (Appendix D) and each participant had full knowledge of this person's involvement. I also included this information in the informed consent.

After I organized the transcripts into meaning units, themes, and descriptive summaries (see the Data Analysis Section for an explanation of this process) I met with each participant a second time to review the information for accuracy. Participants were given an opportunity to read the transcripts and descriptive summaries to vouch for their validity. This ensured what was said during the first interview was in fact captured by the transcript and summary. I also gave participants their own copies of the transcripts and summaries to keep. This demonstrated a person-centered approach and indicated that they were indeed full participants of the process and owned their statements and descriptions of the phenomenon being studied.

The second interview took 60 minutes and was audio taped. At the beginning of this interview I explained what would happen, and the informed consent was reviewed again. This interview gave each participant an opportunity to verify her responses and to clarify her statements. More clarity emerged as participants deepened the meaning of their statements and created more understanding. Also, as I stated earlier, the art making process was introduced during both interviews and, it was not until this second interview that Caroline asked for art supplies while she was clarifying what she had said in the first interview. With oil pastels and paper she drew two images while she verified how she experiences self-doubt in her practice. This process created more description, deepening the understanding of self-doubt, because she was drawing and talking at the same time. In addition, Caroline brought a drawing she had created at home after her first interview. Toward the end of the second interview she described this drawing in full detail expanding the understanding of self-doubt even further because, at this time, she chose a felt marker and created a change in her drawing, demonstrating a deepening of this understanding. During the art making part of the interview I continued to ask open-ended questions to encourage Caroline to explain further the meaning in her drawings. As mentioned, these art images were photographed with her permission and they then became data and were included (see Chapter Four) as a visual record of this participant's experiences of the phenomenon being studied.

While the other three participants did not choose to draw, they each described their experiences and thoughts using metaphorical language. For example, Marcie described her self-doubt with respect to a sand tray she had created before her participation in this inquiry. Tracy spoke of self-doubt being like quicksand, and Penny spoke of two sides of herself. Moreover, this second interview generated more data and another transcript was typed. It too was organized into meaning units and themes, which were then added to the descriptive summaries.

Finally, to thank the participants for their involvement and to share the findings I met with each participant for one final 30-minute follow-up session. I did not audiotape this session. I brought the completed descriptive summaries that captured both interviews and read them aloud to each participant to check for their accuracy. I also explained how I would include the summaries, images, descriptions, and stories of self-doubt, as well as the themes that emerged, in the body of this text.

Data Analysis

Rubin and Rubin (1995) note that "[d]ata analysis is the final stage of listening to hear the meaning of what is said" (p. 226). Therefore, I analyzed the data for the purpose of discovering the meanings and themes of the participants' experiences of self-doubt in the descriptions and stories generated from the interviews. To dissect and reflect on this data I spent much time with it through a deep "in-dwelling" (Junge & Linesch, 1993 and Bentz & Shapiro, 1998) to gain understanding. This means I immersed myself completely in the data generated from the audiotapes, transcripts, research notes, and drawings. While I read and re-read and wrote and re-wrote the data, meaning emerged. I followed Hycner's (1985) guidelines for the phenomenological analysis of interview data, which he based on the works of Colaizzi (1973, 1978), Giorgi (1975), Keen (1975), and Tesch (1980). I followed these steps for all four participants.

First, my typist and I transcribed the 120-minute interview. I noted voice tone, pauses, and non-verbal communication. Second, I suspended (bracketed) my own judgments and entered the world-view of the participant as I listened to the recording and read the transcript again. I remained open to whatever meanings emerged. Third, I listened to the interview once again and re-read the transcript to get a sense of the whole.

Fourth, I noted units of general meaning. Each word, phrase, and sentence in the transcript were re-written to condense what the participant said while still capturing the participant's meaning by using the literal words of the interview. For example, at the start of the first interview Caroline's exact transcript read: "Okay – um…I don't know where to begin… (unsure of self, hesitates)…I started… (pause)…and that makes me five years and that I have more self-doubt right now, because I don't have a lot of experience…(another pause)". These words, phrases, and sentences were written into the following general meaning units: 1. she doesn't know where to begin (unsure of self, hesitates), 2. she started (pause), 3. makes her five years experienced (another pause), and 4. she has more self-doubt now because she has less experience. These general meaning units were written separately from the transcript.

Fifth, I directed the research question: What do child and youth care practitioners experience when they experience self-doubt in their practice? to each general meaning unit. This condensed the general meaning units into relevant meaning units, which noted statements relevant to the research question. For example, the following relevant meaning units were noted from the previous example: 1. she doesn't know where to begin (unsure of self, hesitates) and 2. she has more self-doubt now because she has less experience. The relevant meaning units were also written separately.

Sixth, I looked over the pages of relevant meaning units and eliminated the statements that were redundant. Seventh, I re-read these non-redundant relevant meaning units and grouped them together as they naturally clustered around common themes. For example, I examined each non-redundant relevant meaning unit closely to determine the essence of it, noting whether other meaning units had the same essence. When they did I grouped them together under one common theme. This was a time consuming and difficult process as there was much data to organize and consolidate into common themes.

Eighth, I read and re-read the various clusters of common themes to determine whether these clusters were reflecting a central theme. I then grouped the common themes together under a central theme. For example, the following cluster of common themes, for Caroline, reflected the central theme of coping with self-doubt: taking risks, being self-aware, talking to others, and taking care of self.

Ninth, I wrote a summary of the interview incorporating the non-redundant relevant meaning units and common themes that emerged from the data. The summary also gave a sense of the whole, staying close to the participants' descriptions of the phenomenon. Tenth, in a file folder I gathered each participant's transcript, general meaning units, relevant meaning units, clusters of common themes, grouping of central themes, and the summary, and I met with her to legitimize the stories and descriptions. Hycner (1985) describes this as "[a]n excellent "validity check" . . . to return to the research participant with the written summary and themes and engage in a dialogue with this person concerning what the researcher has found so far" (p. 291). Therefore, the second interview gave each participant an opportunity to clarify and validate her responses as well as acknowledge that the first interview had been accurately and fully captured.

Then, as a result of the second interview steps one through nine were repeated. This process modified the meaning units, common themes, central themes, and summaries, illuminating the phenomenon of self-doubt even further. I met with the participants a third time to legitimize the final summary, to thank them, and to share the results.

Summary

Establishing access, making contact, building relationships, interviewing the participants, transcribing the data, working with the material, analyzing the data, seeking clarity and checking for accuracy, and sharing what I learned, all took on a life of its own. My research design became a living, moving, breathing map as I followed its path in the field. Kvale (1996) likens this process to the traveler on a journey who follows a method of discovering tales and stories to be told, meanings and understandings to be described, and new narratives to be validated. Janesick (1994) suggests, "[t]he design serves as a foundation for the understanding of the participants' worlds and the meaning of shared experiences between the researcher and the participants in a given social context" (p. 210). Thus, my research design offered me the opportunity to share the journey with the participants in a meaningful, purposeful, and ethical way.

Validity

Kvale (1996) notes the validity of qualitative research rests with " . . . issues of truth and knowledge" (p. 236). The *Oxford Dictionary of Current English* (1994) defines *valid* as meaning sound, defensible, and executed with the proper formalities. McNiff (1986) stipulates that "[s]cientific validity is essentially a matter of what people believe to be true, useful, and in their personal interest . . . and [v]alidity and truthfulness relate to the ability of researchers to convince their audiences" (p. 286). Janesick (1994) states that "[v]alidity in qualitative research has to do with description and explanation, and whether or not a given explanation fits a given description. In other words, is the explanation credible?" (p. 216). Seidman (1991) declares that " . . . the goal of the process is to understand how our participants understood and make meaning of their experience. If the interview structure works to allow them to make sense to themselves as well as to the interviewer, then it has gone a long way toward validity" (p. 17).

Thus, the authenticity of what the participant is saying in the interview establishes the validity. For example, on page 42 of this text the meaning unit number 2 (she has more self-doubt now because she has less experience), taken from Caroline's transcript of the first interview, is different from the direct quote to be found on page 50 ("Self-doubt grows more with the more experience I have, not with less experience. The more experience I have in the field the more I notice self-doubt"). This quote is taken from the transcript from the second interview and the reason there is a difference is because, during the second interview, I asked Caroline to explain what she meant when she said she has more self-doubt now because she has less experience. This resulted in Caroline going deeper in her description because Caroline was able to clarify her words and make more meaning of her experience. As a result she and I came to a deeper understanding.

Checking for clarity and inviting the participants to legitimize their words during this second interview allowed me to understand the participants' experiential world more fully and describe how things "really are" for them. I sought a first-person understanding and remained close to each participant's language and descriptions of the phenomenon being studied. I gained a better understanding of what it is like for these four child and youth care practitioners to experience self-doubt in their practice.

According to Pollio, Henley, and Thompson (1997) validity in a phenomenological inquiry is determined by how rigorous and appropriate the procedural structure of the research (methodological concerns) is and how plausible and illuminating the interpretive results (experiential concerns) are. I followed a consistent method of analysis and this helped me to remain faithful to the original transcript. The phenomenon is represented accurately as it occurred during the interviews because the data was read and written over and over again to capture the meaning of what the participants said. Also, I asked the participants to review the transcripts and the summaries to check for accuracy. Further, I used the following techniques to increase credibility: face-to-face interviews, person-centered approach, collaborative interview process, three meetings with the participants over eight months, and telephone contact. Palys (1997) states valid data comes from close and extended contact with research participants. The participants and I constructed knowledge in a systematic, simple, and purposeful way.

The study has generated plausible and illuminating results which contribute to new insights. Plausibility is achieved as the reader sees the relationship between the discoveries, reflections, and the data. The discoveries and reflections are supported by the data in the stories and descriptions. Illumination is achieved as myself and the participants hear and see the phenomenon of self-doubt with new understanding. I also have presented concrete examples of the participants' experiences. Pollio, Henley, and Thompson (1997) note that validity is determined because there is convincing evidence that the thematic description " . . . affords insights into the experiential (lived) world of the participants" (p. 53). In this phenomenological inquiry the phenomenon described is grounded in lived experience and has been accurately reported. The participants gave rich and varied accounts of their experiences of self-doubt in their practice.

Issues related to Phenomenological Research

After conducting phenomenological research I am mindful of performing a research method without an extensive background in philosophy. I prepared myself by reading as much phenomenological literature as I possibly could digest and I was cognizant of using a concrete research method while keeping in mind that the phenomenon and question dictate the method. With so much written on phenomenological research methods I was glad to have found Hycner's (1985) guidelines because they helped me to perform a systematic analysis of phenomenological interview data. Furthermore, in his article, Hycner describes issues that are raised in relation to phenomenological research and I address some of these issues in this section.

First, one of the issues raised has to do with whether or not the results can be generalized. In this inquiry I sought to illuminate the phenomenon of self-doubt in child and youth care practice, not to generalize the findings. Polkinghorne (1989) states the goal of selecting participants, in a phenomenological study, is to obtain rich and varied descriptions, not to achieve statistical generalization. This is the reason why the participants were purposefully selected rather than randomly selected. According to Hycner (1985) when the results are not generalizable, "...they can be phenomenologically informative about human being in general" (p. 295) and "...rigor emerges from the type of participants chosen and their ability to fully describe the experience being researched" (p. 294). Even though the discoveries of this inquiry apply to only the participants interviewed it is valuable to gain insights into the worlds of these participants to illuminate the phenomenon of self-doubt and to encourage others to explore their own experiences.

Another issue is replicability, which means if the same study is performed by another researcher similar discoveries would be found. The replication of a phenomenological inquiry is not recommended as Marshall and Rossman (1999) point out:

> Qualitative research does not claim to be replicable. The researcher purposefully avoids controlling the research conditions and concentrates on recording the complexity of situational contexts and interrelations as they occur naturally. The researcher's goal of discovering this complexity by altering research strategies within a flexible research design, moreover, cannot be replicated by future researchers, nor should it be attempted.
> (p. 195)

Ray (1994) confirms that many researchers have particular attitudes or orientations to phenomenological methodology which derive from their perceptions of philosophical knowledge. Colaizzi (1978) indicates there are many phenomenological methods, and Keen (1975) states " . . . unlike other methodologies, phenomenology cannot be reduced to a "cookbook" set of instructions" (p. 4). Therefore, in phenomenological research it could be conceived that other researchers could view the phenomenon differently because they may be looking at the same data differently due to their perspective, approach, attitude, or, as Keen says, "... investigative posture with a certain set of goals" (p.4). Giorgi (1975) suggests:

> ... the chief point to be remembered with this type of research is not so much whether position with respect to the data could be adopted ... but whether a reader, adopting the same viewpoint as articulated by the researcher, can also see what the researcher saw, whether or not he agrees with it. (p. 96)

Thus, I believe I followed the principles of conducting a phenomenological inquiry that is both valid and ethical. I challenged myself as I came to a philosophical understanding of phenomenology and bracketed my own personal experiences of the phenomenon of self-doubt. I received rich and varied descriptions from the participants and extrapolated meaning and understanding. Paul (1999) eloquently states:

> As qualitative technique, phenomenology is unique because the involvement of the participants extends beyond the interview process. Phenomenology is essentially a project of discovery; for the researcher, to elucidate the structure of the phenomenon of interest, and for the participants an opportunity to explore a significant experience. Most importantly, it reveals our ability to think in a phenomenological manner, to examine the ordinary experiences and discover within them that which is extraordinary. (p. 202)

CHAPTER FOUR
Presentation of the Data

In times of self-doubt and despair all of life appears unreal, false, dishonest, even brutal. Then one day you find someone who listens ...someone gentle who feels your presence and you start gradually to exist again, to feel, to trust, to be a genuine person. You begin to believe in life and to live, without rancor or fear, in the midst of joy and beauty and friendship. The tragedy is over and you have been born anew. Life takes on a sense of permanency. In the midst of this passion for life, there is continuing sense of self-realizing.

Clark Moustakas (1967, p.124)

After I listened to the voices of the participants and condensed the data I wrote summaries of the interviews and divided them into stories and descriptions. The participants validated the content of these summaries and they reflect each participant's unique language. The stories and descriptions portray the world of each participant as it was presented to me during the interviews. I begin this chapter with describing the stories and descriptions of self-doubt, followed by listing the common and central themes in a table, and ending with a discussion of my discoveries and impressions.

Stories of Self-Doubt

  Caroline's story.

During the interviews Caroline spoke clearly, yet slowly, with much hesitation and many pauses as if to give much thought to what she would say. She had difficulty knowing how to begin the first interview. She started by talking about the years of experience she has had in the field. In the beginning she says she was unclear as to how she wanted to perform according to her own standards (expectations), and with more experience she has begun to develop a standard for how she wants to work.

The more experience she has in the field, the more she is aware of the self-doubt in her practice. She says, "Self-doubt grows more with the more experience I have, not with less experience. The more experience I have in the field the more I notice self-doubt." For example, she usually experiences self-doubt when she has difficulty making a decision in her work with clients or when she questions the decisions after she has made them. She then becomes unsure of herself, second-guesses herself, and wonders, "Did I go about that in the right way? Did it (the decision) help our relationship move forward? Did I react in the right way? I did not do this and the client is not responding, therefore, what kind of work have I done with the client if I do not see any results right away?"

When she has "bad" days at work her self-doubt is bigger because the rewards are less (when she does not receive acknowledgement or praise from her co-workers or supervisor or does not have a personal feeling of accomplishment). For example, she says, "It's okay to venture in (to look within herself), but I do find I get lost when I'm in self-doubt. It takes away…(pause)…I don't have as much access to my energy. Or, I'm not thinking clearly. It's kind of like being in a fog."

She has less self-doubt when she is feeling "good" about the job she is doing. Feeling good about the job comes from having a rewarding feeling inside that what she has done at work has meaning beyond simply being told what to do from her employer. She says, "There's got to be something there. There's got to be a sense of accomplishment. In my job when I'm feeling good about myself and good about what I'm doing then I question myself less. I have less self-doubt when I'm feeling good about the job that I do. And feeling good about that job comes from having a good…having a rewarding…ah…I…I…I don't want to put the good and bad labels on anything, but having that feeling inside that what I've done at work is…(pause)…had some meaning beyond…beyond doing what I've been told what I've got to do. It meant something to somebody."

She says not seeing or feeling the rewards of her job just might be the kind of job this (child and youth care) is and it can be harder to see past the fog of self-doubt to a place where there is more light. She also says it is important for her to feel valued in her work. Specifically she says, "Hmmm, you know, maybe I could be doing something else and maybe I would be doing…I would be accomplishing something else and it's not seeing or feeling the rewards of the job and maybe that's just the way this kind of job is, where there's some days, where, you know, it's… ahh…a rewardless kind of work, where, you know, it's YUCK! YUCK! YUCK! And it can be harder to see the light. And, I think that has less to do with the people I'm working with and more to do with how, you know, what's going on for me, you know. But when they're (clients) not doing so well and I'm not doing so well, and I'm kind of looking and saying to myself, 'why am I doing this type of work again?' "

When Caroline is experiencing self-doubt on the job she asks herself a lot of questions: "Am I good working here?" "Is anybody else going to hire me?" "What do I have to offer?" "What am I doing here?" "Why am I in this job?" "What can I offer people?" "Did I go about it the right way?" "Did I react in the right way?" "Did I cross boundaries?" "Did I do something that the youth are fully capable of doing themselves?" "Am I doing the right thing in this situation?"

Further, Caroline says that when she takes care of herself better she is able to have a balance between her self-care and self-doubt. She says, "In order to have less self-doubt I need to…umm…get stronger within myself. When I'm taking care of myself. When I've had enough sleep and rest and, you know, my house is in order, so to speak, where, you know, where I've taken care of all my business at home and my personal life seems to be good, and…ummm… and then at work when…when I've done something well…when I'm feeling good about myself and good about what I'm doing at work I question and doubt myself less."

She also feels self-doubt physically in her body. She says, "What happens for me is a restriction in my body. A tightening…umm…and umm…a frown. My eyebrows will come together and…umm (sigh)…there's not a lot of room for creativity. That's the other part of self-doubt. There's no vibrancy or creativity for life. It's just an existing…it blocks the creativity to make those creative decisions to get around obstacles. It really…it really…umm…paralyzes me." She also is concerned about pleasing others and doing it right. She likes to go the "extra mile" for her clients (for example, give her clients a ride somewhere) and then wonders after if it was the right thing to do because maybe she has done too much for them. She says, "Maybe I have done something that they (clients) were fully capable of doing."

At one point in her career feelings of self-doubt would have stopped her from taking risks. She says, "As I've gone along in my practice I take more risks now than I did before. I have a bit of experience and with this foundation I say to myself, 'well, okay, just try something different'…so at one point there could have been self-doubt that would stop me from trying something new and now with more experience on the job, self-doubt keeps me open to new experiences." She explains further, "It becomes a place to take a risk, you know, when I have so much more inner resources (her experience, energy, values, beliefs, and boundaries) and then there's that little bit of self-doubt that will be enough to pique my curiosity to say to myself, 'Why do I have doubt about that? And what would happen if I decided to do it anyways?' I think there's enough inner resources in me to fall back on that if it were…if it didn't work out then I say, 'Okay, we can move on to the next thing. It didn't work and there's a lesson and there's a risk, and I've learned something regardless of whether it worked out the way I thought it should or not'."

When she experiences less self-doubt she knows her inner resources better and this is a place where she can take more risks in her work. She says in the beginning, she did not connect her work with her inner resources enough: "I think back to the beginning of the job when I was eager and new and felt I could do anything and I hadn't made any mistakes...um...or I hadn't really internalized my process. I hadn't connected my work with my inner process (what was going on inside of her)." Now she finds she is more self-aware about her inner resources. She has come to know her own boundaries, values, and beliefs and how these affect her self-doubt. She experiences positive self-doubt when she keeps herself open to new experiences. She has learned to trust taking risks in her work as she has learned from her self-doubts and her experiences. She says, "What happens over time is that I get to know my own boundaries and I become aware of my own values with regard to work that...umm...that's where more confidence can be built and...umm...the self-doubt will seem...it will appear...it's appearing to be less."

In her day-to-day practice she finds she is missing the opportunity to bounce ideas and questions off another person because she often works in isolation and would like to connect with another co-worker immediately when she experiences doubt in her work. By talking about her self-doubt with others, she has a greater understanding of its source. She says, " By talking about it I had a greater understanding of where my doubt came from, like if it came from not doing the right thing or is it about boundaries? Another person can encourage me to talk more about what is behind my self-doubt." In fact Caroline stated she found drawing the pictures of self-doubt and talking about them during the interviews gave her a greater understanding of what self-doubt means to her as she says, "I have a greater sense of what self-doubt means to me now."

Marcie's story.

During the interviews Marcie spoke in a clear, soft, and gentle voice, with little hesitation. She began by describing an experience of working with a family. When she is working with a family sometimes the complexity and the challenges that the family faces seem so huge that she feels ill equipped to make a difference. It seems that the things she is working on with a family are so big that she feels doubt about what she can do and is uncertain about where to begin. Sometimes she feels a little shy or she holds back a little, and when she does this she will often second-guess herself. For example, when she confronted a parent this person became very angry and in the moment she had absolute clarity that she had done the right thing, yet after, she doubted herself when she became aware she was upset by what had happened.

When there is chaos in a family and she has been invited to be a support, there are others expecting milestones to be met. She says, "When I have been invited to be a support person for a family there are other people expecting these milestones to be met…so whose work is it to do? Is it me because I am there? Who's being monitored and how do you get to that place of…ummm…family support that is effective and that has…is measurable? That's what we're called to do is be measurable. Everything has to be accountable and it's all about target outcomes and so the whole funding base of a program is based on that and that's a lot of pressure to go in and say you're trying to be like a coach and these people could have any number of reasons why they're not in shape so how can the game start if they're maybe not even equipped to be on the field. It's going to take some time and there is a time pressure that's imposed."

This is a time in her practice when she feels doubt. She wonders if she is doing a good job and whether she is "inspiring the family". Does she know enough and is she acting in a way that is meeting all the expectations that are put on her by others? These expectations come from her own personal code of ethics, her contractor, her job description, and the culture of the family she is working with at the time. The funding source of a program is based on accountability and measurable outcomes and this is a lot of pressure placed on her, when a family can have any number of reasons why it is "not in shape". She wonders how she can get to that place of family support that is effective and measurable by a specific amount of time. Sometimes she feels like she is "walking on a tightrope" as she feels pulled in several directions – the parents, the child, and the funding source.

She also feels the pressure of being a professional who is expected to do the right thing for a family. She does not see herself as an expert and wonders if she is doing a good enough job. She asks herself whether she is doing enough for the family according to the expectations of everyone involved, including herself. This not "good enough feeling" is her own struggle of thinking she is letting people down. Sometimes she feels she will be rejected by others when they find out she does not know something. She says, "Because…ahh…for me I feel that I could let them (a family) down. That I could not be enough or do enough. I will think that it's…ahh…fear…fear of being …possibility of being rejected."

When she experiences self-doubt she feels it in her body. Physically, she will "shake like a leaf", feel flushed and clammy, and have raised or hunched shoulders. Emotionally, she will cry and/or feel anxious and/or sad. Cognitively, she will ask herself if she is holding her heart, if she is relaxed, or if her voice is deep. She wonders too if most of the self-doubts are just what she has created in her own mind. Nevertheless, she wants to give equal time to the physical, intellectual, and emotional responses. Her body will give her clear messages when she is experiencing self-doubt in her practice. She says, "I can certainly acknowledge the feelings and I am becoming much more aware of my own response…my physiological response, intellectual response, and my emotional response. I'm very interested in the fact that my body will give me very clear messages if I pay attention."

Marcie's self-doubt is influenced by her childhood. She feels that when she was growing up she was to set a good example because her father was a teacher in a small community. She said she was watched a lot by others and she felt others put expectations on her, therefore, she did not want to disappoint these people. She finds it is important to please people and to go the "extra mile" for others in her practice. She presents her "sunshine" side more often than the side that experiences self-doubts (her dark side) because she wants to be accepted and liked by others, not rejected by them.

Marcie reflects on her practice often and this helps her to take risks in her work. She questions herself, wondering what she could have done differently. Her inner dialogue is made up of questions to help her determine whether her self-doubt is based on a phantom fear or a realistic fear. The questions she asks herself include: "Is this something I SHOULD do?" "Is there a benefit for others, for me?" "What will it cost me (in time, energy)?" "If there is fear, what is the fear and what would happen if that fear came true?" "What would be the worst case scenario?" "Is it a realistic fear or a phantom fear?" She wants to feel the doubt, recognize it, and take more risks. She faces her fear and doubt and goes beyond it. Her resolve is strengthened when she moves forward and works with her doubt from a positive perspective. She can make a choice to stretch herself and go beyond the doubt, rather than staying stuck.

She says the best way to nurture herself is to be tuned in to all aspects (layers) of herself and to operate from a more authentic place. She tells herself it is okay for her to acknowledge the parts of herself that are not the "sunshine" parts and that this does not make her any less of a person or less accepted by others. She can put the self-doubt to rest and not need to feel responsible for another person's feelings, positive or negative, because she is being faithful to her own self and she is taking care of herself well. She is paying more attention to what is going on for her on the inside and less attention to the expectations that are coming from the outside. It is a "life lesson" for her.

She acknowledges that learning about and knowing self-doubt is tiring and hard work! She can look at self-doubt in the eye and identify what she is feeling and discover what it is telling her. She says, "And so I can look it (self-doubt) in the eye and just say, 'that's what I'm feeling right now'. And there will be more lessons to learn and the self-doubt is just saying, even if I lose my balance, and it seems like I'm not, like, moving forward if I didn't, if I didn't try anything then I'd never move anywhere! It's okay to take those first steps."

Self-doubt has sparked her to do things differently, to ask the questions that need to be asked, and to find the answers that need to be found. She would love to have a sunny day every single day and yet she knows that she would not have the "expansion that her self-doubts have given her". She has more self-awareness and knows herself better and can recognize her triggers and take the steps to work through them from a human and a professional perspective. She says, "In my sand-tray I placed a shell that held all the echoes of the memories of the waves of goodness that has come into my life and beside this a head of a monster who had very sharp teeth and eyes that were really piercing. And I put them absolutely side by side because I think both of them are really significant. Both of them have influenced and shaped who I am and that the dark side and the sadness and the sorrow (the self-doubts)…umm…is as much a part of what has created and developed me as a human being as the goodness in my life."

Tracy's story.

During the interviews Tracy spoke in a clear, animated, and loud voice and described her experiences very matter-of-factly and metaphorically with lots of enthusiasm.

Tracy began by describing an experience in the field. She held a child and youth care position, which lacked a clear job description or clear expectations. She described going into a slump where everything started to go wrong. She went into a hole, which was a place where she began to tell herself that she should not have taken the job and she was not meant to be in the position. She lost her confidence. She did not understand her role, and she did not know what her place was in the job. She did not trust anyone and she did not know where she belonged and what she should be doing. In fact, she stopped performing in this job all together. She was in "full sulk-mode", and she did not know how to ask for help. Soon the duties of her position were taken away from her and she internalized this message to mean that she was not capable; that she was not doing a good enough job.

When Tracy doubts herself in her practice it means she does not know where to go next or what to do next. She does not know what the steps are period! She does not have a plan and this feeling of not knowing "paralyzes" her. She begins to believe she is not good enough. It is a self-fulfilling prophecy that goes around and around in her head. She believes she is inadequate. She says, "It (to doubt herself in practice) means I don't know where to go next and I don't know what to do next. I don't have a plan…ummm…I don't know what the steps are. I don't even know the steps in the wrong order! I just don't have any sense what the steps are period! It's one thing to…to have a list…to have an idea in your mind that I got to do XY and Z and not know…not know what to do first. At least you have a starting point there…you can go and ask someone, 'Okay, I think I have to do this, this, and this. Have I missed anything?' But if you don't even know where…where…where to start you can't even do that because you just end up paralyzed or at least that's what I would do. This place of not knowing is a terrible place for me!" When she does not know she then becomes moody, irritable, and irresponsible. She feels fear. Self-doubt is an internal feeling, a physical sensation, a bodily reaction. She feels it in her stomach and in her chest. It is a frightening sensation. It is worse than butterflies in her stomach. It is nausea and she feels like she is going to be sick.

Tracy believes if she is good enough, and does a good job, people will like her. She looks for approval in her relationships because she likes to please people. She thinks if she does not please people she will let them down. She thinks she must be five times as good, to be seen as equal to everybody else, because she needs to measure up to the expectations of others. This began in childhood when she learned she needed to measure up to her mother, who is bright, articulate, intelligent, incredibly competent, and very well respected in her field. Perfect people are impossible to measure up to she says, because all they do is make her feel badly about herself, and doubt herself even more. Growing up with a disability taught her to overcompensate as well. She took on the label of hero and became the "standard bearer" of people with disabilities. She says, "I had this belief that I was a hero. I was supposed to be the hero. That was the role I was supposed to play, but in order to be that, in order to fulfill that, I had to be perfect. But I couldn't be perfect, so how could I play the role, but I had to play the role, because THAT WAS MY ROLE!! That is my…that is what I was given, you know. It is like a life position: I am the hero, you know. I mean I've been given that label so many times and it became about turning that around to maybe the hero isn't the one who is perfect."

She says on the one hand it is an honour for her to be a hero and she wants to live up to the role, yet on the other hand she does not want to have the pressure of needing to measure up for heroes are perfect and they do not make mistakes. She says there is a cognitive dissonance between being a hero, being a role model, and being perfect, because she is *not* perfect and she wants to make mistakes! Suddenly she started to think differently, "Oh maybe heroes do screw up. Maybe the hero is the one who soldiers on through the imperfections! Maybe heroes do make mistakes and this is a good thing!" For her, it has been a process of slowly accepting that she is not perfect and she can still be a hero and be comfortable in her "own skin" with her own doubts and imperfections.

The clearer the boundaries are and the clearer the relationships she has with people, the less self-doubt she experiences. She needs to know what the parameters are in her practice. She needs to know where the walls are, where the boundaries are, and where the box is, so that she can determine how far she can go in her work. When her boundaries are tight and clear, and there is no confusion, there is no place to get lost.

Trust is another important ingredient in her work which helps her get through the doubts. She needs to know people trust her then she can make mistakes and take risks. If she cannot trust someone she cannot figure out how to get the person's approval. She also needs to have trust before she can tell someone she is experiencing doubts in her work.

Talking to others helps her work through her self-doubt. She needs to receive "outside" feedback. There needs to be a mirror which will reflect information back to her about herself. She needs support from others and when she is stuck in the quicksand of self-doubt she needs someone she trusts to throw her a rope to help her get out.

When she is feeling self-doubt in her practice she asks herself questions. This inner dialogue helps her to sort out what she needs to do for herself. Whether she needs to face the fear of her doubts and "do it anyway" or whether she needs to think of "worst-case scenarios", the self-talk helps her to discover what is going on for her. Her inner dialogue includes: "Okay, I am having some doubts here." "What am I going to do with this self-doubt?" "Do I need to talk to someone?" "Do I need to feel the fear and do it anyway?" "Do I push through the self-doubt and just do it or do I need some help?" "Is this self-doubt a signal I have taken a chunk that is too big for me?" "What if I fail?" "This could happen and that could happen." "It will be as bad as World War III!!!" "What is the worst thing that can really happen?" "Have I got everything here?"

Humour is an important characteristic of Tracy's personality. In a previous job she lost sight of her humour and this experience taught her when the self-doubt is too big, she is not able to see it from a humourous perspective. She cannot "lighten it up" or "make a joke of it". Humour will help her shift or move the self-doubt when she is feeling stuck. Humour is something more active than just sitting there "sucking her thumb", sulking and being in "victim mode". Humour brings her out of that place of feeling "not good enough!"

Having faith also helps her deal with her self-doubts. She believes God needs her to experience "some stuff" in her life to help her get to where she needs to go. She believes it is all part of some journey and process of fulfilling some destiny. She realizes she is not there yet, as she is still on the journey. Faith helps her become stronger so she can look at the self-doubt that "paralyzes" her. She recognizes she needs to let go of the control and, with faith, allow things to just happen the way they are meant to happen in her life.

Self-awareness is important to Tracy because it helps her to recognize what the self-doubt is, so she can discover what she needs to learn about herself. She needs to be "in touch" with her self-doubt and be "in contact" with it so she can work through it. She describes this as working with her self-doubt in a healthy way. When she responds to self-doubt in an active, positive, and healthy way, she uses it as a force for change and growth, then she says self-doubt is a good teacher because she is open to learning something new about herself.

Tracy says, "I think there's negative self-doubt and there's positive self-doubt." Positive self-doubt is the "warning bells". It makes her double-check her procedures in her work. Has she dotted all the "Is" and crossed all the "Ts"? This is best practice, she says, as it is important for her to follow procedures and know how "to do things right" in her work, because it could determine the fate of a child or youth's care. Healthy self-doubt is not being afraid to ask the questions, to do a mental check of steps, or to ask for help and talk to another colleague when she is feeling some doubts in her work.

When she is experiencing negative self-doubt she is experiencing the "paralyzing kind". It leaves her sulking and victimized in quicksand. She is "stuck in the muck" and this is not a useful or productive place for her to be in her practice. Tracy is reminded of "Gregor", a cockroach character in the short story "Metamorphosis" by Franz Kafka. She compares her negative experience of self-doubt with the cockroach in the story, which keeps moving in circles. The more Tracy moves in circles, the more the self-doubt consumes her and takes over her life. Stories like this help remind her about learning important lessons in her professional life.

Penny's story.

During the interviews Penny spoke in a soft and gentle voice with lots of pauses as she found the words to describe her experiences. Penny experiences self-doubt daily in her work. She will experience self-doubt before, during, or after a situation with a client. Often, after a day on the job, she goes home and second-guesses herself, thinking about what she could have said or done differently. She sometimes compares herself with others, noting sometimes she does not feel as effective. For example, when she starts a new job she has less confidence. She says, "If I doubt myself then I can get into a…ummm…a negative thinking versus positive thinking."

When Penny experiences self-doubt she also becomes very emotional and experiences bodily reactions such as having difficulties breathing, feeling sick to her stomach, or a tightness in her chest or abdomen. She experiences anxious feelings, stressful feelings, and panic attacks. Sometimes she cannot sleep at night.

Regardless of what she is feeling on the inside, Penny does carry on with her work, showing the outer confident part of herself more often than her inner, unsure self. She is learning to be more congruent in her work as she believes it is important for her to be aware and learn from her "inner stuff". When she knows herself and her role in her job better, she feels more comfortable with what she is doing and this helps to lessen the self-doubt. With each experience of working with people she deepens her understanding of self-doubt within her practice.

Penny grew up expecting a lot from herself and this has carried over into her work. She wants to be the best she can be and she wants to be as helpful as she can be. She needs to be prepared, organized, and confident. She wants to be more present with her self-doubt as this will help her to be more congruent in her work. She needs to be patient with herself so that she can learn all the things she needs to know. When she is able to separate what is a realistic and achievable expectation, from what is not, she will be able to resolve the negative feelings of thinking she cannot do something.

When other people tell Penny what to do she feels judged. She thinks she must do things a certain way or the right way according to how other people do it or how others say it is to be done. She wants to be liked by others, therefore she wants to do it "their way", even though inside she feels she cannot be creative or make mistakes. When the work environment is full of judgments from others and lots of talk about the right way and wrong way of doing things, then she experiences more self-doubt that is debilitating. Some of the questions she asks herself include: Am I smart enough? Am I cut out for this? What will people think of me? Her inner dialogue includes both negative and positive self-talk. For example:

<u>Negative self-talk</u>
"I cannot do this!"
"What do I have to contribute?"
"Why am I in this field?"
"Why do I think I can do this?"
"Can I work with people?"
"Can I counsel people?"
"I do not know if I can do that."
"Look at how skilled that person is or look at how much that person knows."
"That did not go well."

<u>The positive self-talk reframes the negative.</u>
"I *can* do this."
"There is a reason why I am in this job – I was hired – I am capable – I have schooling."
"What is *really* happening?"
"I am way out of my comfort zone and I am taking a risk. What do I need?"
"I will know next time."
"I will check *that* out."
"I have dealt with that better."
"I am still learning." "This is a process."
"This is part of building relationships."

When she is fearful or when she puts herself down too much, she sees the self-doubt as negative. When the self-doubt becomes negative it is debilitating and she gets stuck. She sees negative self-doubt as a huge thing. For example, sometimes she makes mountains out of mole-hills. She becomes defensive and wonders if she is in the right profession. Sometimes she feels devastated. She loses her voice and cannot speak up about what she believes or values. The maladaptive thoughts have taken over and she believes there is something wrong with her. On the other hand, self-doubt can be positive. It is a healthy thing for her to always examine how she is doing things. Questioning how she can be more articulate, more professional, more helpful, or more skillful is positive. She can make changes within herself and can deal with things better next time. She learns from her mistakes. Questioning how she does things brings more clarity into her practice. Reflecting deepens her understanding of self-doubt. She can recognize that she is still an okay person even though she has feelings of self-doubt. It is important for her to separate self-doubt from her self-esteem. Naming the self-doubt helps her to identify what is going on for her and what she needs. Self-doubt can enhance her professional ethics and practice. Self-doubt pushes her to try harder and do better in her work. When she is open to looking at the scared feelings of self-doubt within herself she learns to not "hide" them from others.

Talking to others also helps her to sort out what is going on for her. A strong support network helps her to deal with her feelings of self-doubt. She likes to bounce ideas off another person. When she talks to others about the field of child and youth care she finds it helps her to become clearer about the profession. Her self-doubt becomes more manageable and workable. She also likes to hear what other people experience as it helps her feel less alone. When she shares her inadequacies with others she is more accepting of herself.

She learns more when she receives feedback from others. It helps to get a glimpse in the mirror of her "backside" to help her uncover some of the difficult feelings she has about herself. When she gathers more self-awareness and more experience she learns more about her self-doubt. Being aware of her thought patterns and processes helps her to identify what triggers her self-doubt in her practice. Working on herself brings more understanding into her work. She says, "I struggle with self-doubt all the time, but I think that, as I feel more comfortable and know my roles and what I'm doing, then I think that it (self-doubt) lessens even more and then I just feel more confident about myself. One of the things that I've found a theme that keeps coming up is that here I was saying, 'I can't do this. I'm not smart enough.' But then I thought, 'You know, I get into this type of thinking and then it's almost like a self-fulfilling prophecy of: I don't do well or I don't do as well as I could have.' But if I back away from it (the negative thinking and doubting) I start to think I *can* do this! And I *have* been doing it!! And it's strange and then I try and get out of the cycle of thinking this way. I'm starting to really challenge myself and that's where I've…I think I've become aware over the last say four or five months that, that *is* a cycle that I can get into, or a pattern of thinking and I'm still trying to work through that. I'm trying to look at it (self-doubt) from a different perspective."

Penny has developed some inner resources which help her to understand her self-doubt. She reads more so she can think about her practice more. She tries to change her way of thinking or how she approaches a situation more positively to help her overcome the debilitating kind of self-doubt. She gives herself positive affirmations to build her self-esteem. She taps into her inner strengths and natural skills. She writes in her journal to try to figure out what is going on with the turmoil she feels on the inside. She gets to a place of calm. She becomes more comfortable with who she is. She forges through the self-doubt that gets her stuck. She takes care of herself better and knows herself better.

Finally, Penny believes there is a need for some healthy self-doubt to keep her humble. With distance, time, patience, awareness, and understanding she is able to work through the experiences of self-doubt in her practice. She says, "But I think it (self-doubt) will be an ongoing thing for me. I don't think I'll get over it. There has to be some healthy self-doubt in there (little laugh) you know keeps me humble. I'm so emotionally tied to it (self-doubt) so if I'm able to express that to somebody else they can feed back what they see and it helps me to get some distance from it, some patience, understanding, awareness."

Descriptions of Self-Doubt

Caroline's description.

During the second interview, Caroline described her self-doubt as a road coming closer and closer together. She says on one side of the road is her internal experience and on the other side is her perception of the external experience. With more experience, in the field, the roads come closer together and with less experience the roads are farther apart. Self-doubt is in between these two roads. At this point in the interview, Caroline pauses in her verbal description and chooses purple, orange, and grey pastels to draw what she is describing.

In her first drawing (figure 4.1) Caroline drew the internal experience, which she identified as her personal values, with an orange pastel. Next, she drew the external experience, which she identified as her perception of societal and organizational expectations, with a purple line. She coloured the space between the orange and purple lines with the grey pastel. She says this is her self-doubt. She says there is more self-doubt (grey) when the internal and external (orange and purple lines) are farther apart. Suddenly, she realizes she should have drawn something else and chose another piece of paper.

In her second drawing (figure 4.2) the external experience stays the same and she showed this by drawing a straight purple line. She says the external experience is out of her control. The internal experience represents her values, beliefs, boundaries, and self-esteem. Her internal experience starts at the top of the paper and moves down the paper on a gradual slope. She showed this by drawing a curved line in orange. In the beginning, when she started to work in the field she was not very aware of her values and beliefs and the external expectations seemed very far away from her internal process. She thinks she will be in the wider part of self-doubt (grey) for a while yet in this profession, as she is still learning. She knows she can get stronger within herself so that she will have less self-doubt and this comes with more experience in the field. When her internal experience (orange line) is parallel with the external experience (purple line) she has less doubt as a practitioner because she values herself more.

Caroline chose orange for her internal experience because it is bright, colourful, and warm. She chose purple for the external expectations because it is bold. The two colours compliment each other and are equal in intensity. She chose grey for self-doubt because it is fuzzy, not clear, not black nor white, because it is somewhere in between. Grey is a dull, passive colour which reminds her of being lost and in a fog.

It is okay for her to be in the self-doubt (grey) when she can see her expectations clearly and she can see her own internal compass or lighthouse. She gets lost in the self-doubt (grey) when she does not have as much access to her energy (her internal experience). She is not thinking clearly and it is like being in a fog. When she is lost in the fog she is further away from her internal experience and her internal sense of knowing she can do something. When the internal (orange) and the external (purple) lines are closer together she feels more congruent and her work is more rewarding. This is the time she feels good about her work and she enjoys what she is doing. She says, "I love my job!" The grey makes her think cold, clouds, fog, and "Brrr". Cold makes her think restriction, where warmth is expansion.

Following this explanation she filled in the space above the orange line with more orange colour (figure 4.3). The external experience is constant and stays the same so she fills in the space with more purple colour. It makes the self-doubt smaller because there is a whole lot of orange (internal experience) in this space now. Sometimes the self-doubt can take over her whole internal experience and that is when it feels like a big fog, when she is in the wide part of the grey space. When this happens there is less orange colour (less internal experience). In the fog things do not look as bright and the world does not have the same kind of shine or sparkle. Self-doubt blocks the vibrancy and the creativity because she cannot access or see her internal resources to make those creative decisions to get around obstacles in her work. This is when self-doubt paralyzes her in the field. At this point, in the interview, Caroline referred to her third drawing (figure 4.4), which was drawn after her first interview. This drawing is about being in the self-doubt; in the grey part when it is paralyzing her. There are many different coloured question marks in the middle of the page. Beside each question mark is a letter. It is like being in a fog when it is difficult to see because it is difficult to see the letters spelling out the words. "Fear" is spelled out in red felt marker, which is the easiest to see. The other blue and green letters spell "right", "wrong", "confusion", "valued", and "opinion". At the bottom there is a purple eye which represents what she is seeing. At the top there is a yellow light bulb which represents ideas and opportunities. The question marks are like this ball of confusion. Sometimes when there are too many questions and too much confusion in the middle there is no vision of what lies beyond the confusion, which are the ideas and the opportunities (the light bulb). Outside the confusion are arrows pointing outward, indicating the confusion could go out and get bigger.

When there is less confusion, less fog, less self-doubt, the eye gets bigger, therefore, she can see more internal resources, more opportunities, and her own valued opinions. Fear and confusion are in the middle, at the core of self-doubt. Fear in red stands out because it gets the "ball rolling" (fuels the self-doubt). She experiences fear of being wrong, of not being good enough, of not measuring up. The arrows symbolize directions and after she recognizes this she makes an adjustment to her drawing creating another point on the arrow showing the arrows going both ways (inward as well as out). The self-doubt moves in and out and can be small or big. As the self-doubt gets smaller the light bulb appears bigger and brighter. In the fog (self-doubt) she has difficulty seeing the light bulb (her inner resources, ideas, and opportunities). When the fog lifts she can see the light (inner resources) more clearly. The light of the light bulb reminds her of a lighthouse, which is the symbol of hope.

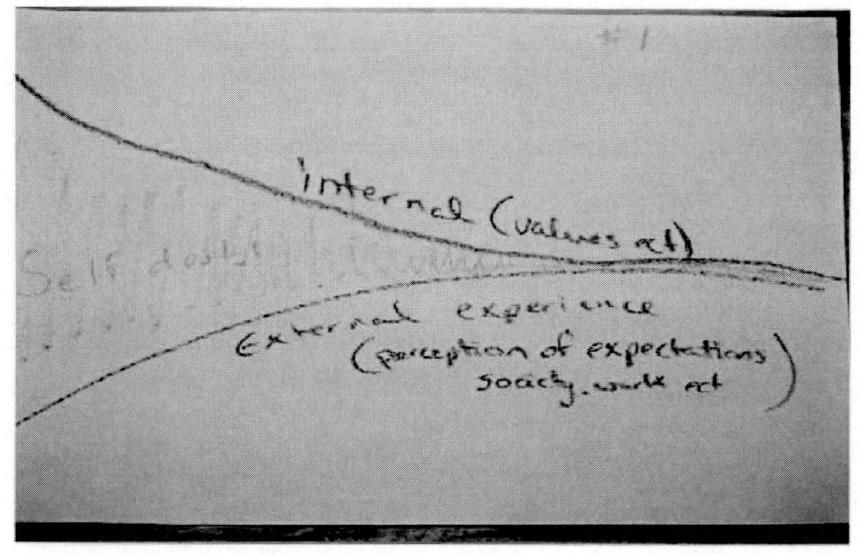

Figure 4.1

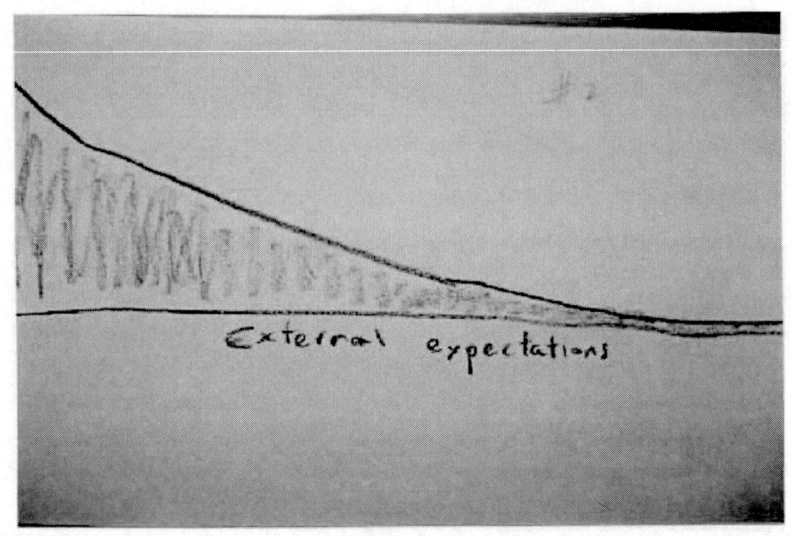

Figure 4.2

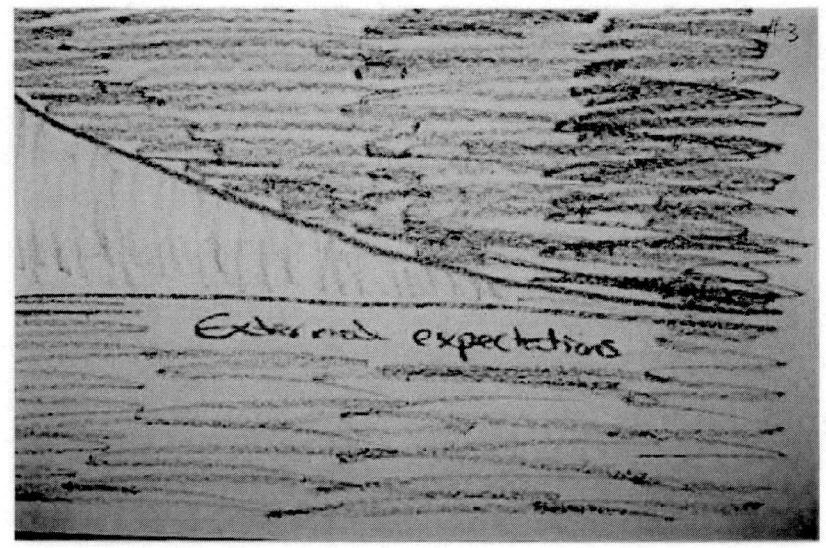

Figure 4.3

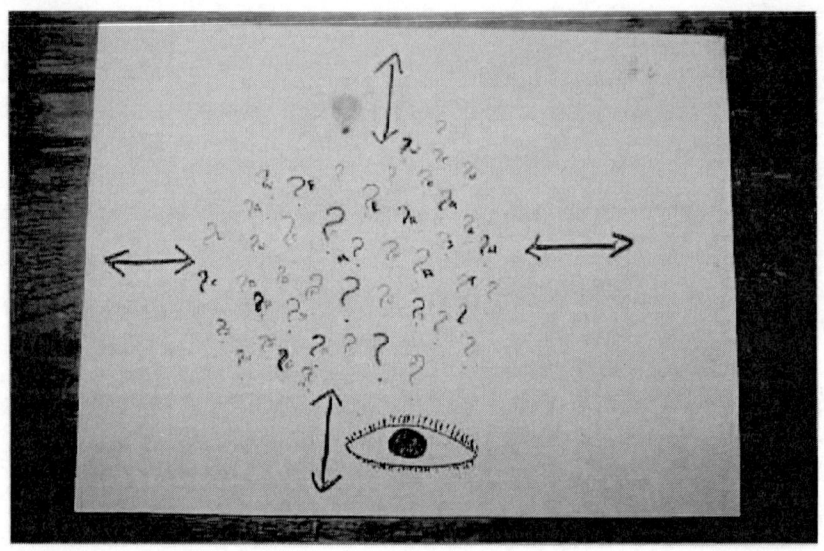

Figure 4.4

Marcie's description.

During the second interview, Marcie explained what self-doubt looks like and means to her by describing a sand-tray she made, several months before the interview, while she was taking a counselling course. She first began by making a mountain in the sand. The mountain was before her and on top of this mountain she put some trees, which were made from mirrors. The image that she created for herself was that of a Hopi Indian Storyteller. She made a path and placed herself halfway up the mountain because she is 46, so she figured her life is half over. She has come this far and she is striving to reach the top of the mountain. The top of the mountain represents the end of her life on earth and the beginning of her life in eternity. The trees on top of this mountain represent the Father, the Son, and the Holy Spirit. She made certain that the mirrors on the trees would reflect her present and her past.

Right behind her she placed the shell of a moon snail, which she half-buried in the sand. This shell holds all the echoes of the memories of the waves of goodness that have come into her life. Partnering the shell she placed an image of a huge head of a monster with very sharp teeth and piercing eyes. The shell and the monster are side by side because both are very significant in her life, as both have influenced and shaped who she is. The monster represents her dark side (sadness, self-doubts) and she feels it is as much a part of what has created and developed her as a human being. Both of these images (shell and monster) were reflected in the mirrors. She was not trying to hide this dark side of herself or the darkness she has experienced in her life. She often dances with her dark side, her self-doubt.

She also placed some clear glass stones on the path. These stones represent some of the jewels she has gathered and some yet to come. The jewels are highlighted moments in her life and things she has accomplished. These jewels were shining in the sand and she always wants to reflect on them. She pushed some of the sand away to reveal blue reflecting water. The water is an image of a river which represents the flow of her life, because her energy, her ideas, and who she is will still be reflected on this earth even when her river ends. She feels the image of the water brings much strength and calmness, like finding a place of balance between calm and action, light and dark; striving forward and being in a time of rest. There are layers of herself and each layer reflects what is underneath. She can see all the different aspects of herself – the playful, the storyteller, the active, the quiet, the dark, the light, the capable and the doubtful. She strives for balance in her life and work.

Tracy's description.

Tracy's descriptions of her self-doubt evolved during both interviews. She compares her self-doubt to a "mushroom cloud", like an atomic bomb in World War III. Self-doubt means second-guessing herself. It is the fear of not knowing she can do something. This feeling is a terrible and uncomfortable place for her. When she has self-worth she can deal with the self-doubt. When she has no sense of self-worth, the self-doubt becomes a "Paralyzing Blob" that she cannot get through. It is like being in quicksand of which she does not know how to get out. The more she tries to fight the self-doubt (the quicksand) the more she sinks into it. The fears, the questions, and the doubts all build up on each other. She begins to think too much, imagining the worst ("catastrophyzing"), and this results in her sinking deeper into the quicksand (self-doubt). Then she feels very sorry for herself and she begins to sulk, which she identifies as being in "victim mode" or "full sulk mode".

Over time, Tracy has learned that being in too much quicksand is not a healthy place for her. She also has found a mentor in her life, which has helped her work through the strong feelings of self-doubt she has experienced in her work.

She recognizes there has been some important lessons she has learned and some yet to learn.

Penny's description.

Penny's descriptions of her self-doubt also evolved during both interviews. She depicts her self-doubt as always questioning herself. Does she know enough? What could she have done differently? Does she have enough education? Self-doubt is about doubting her ability and what she has to offer. She feels less confident and not good about herself when she starts a new job. She says, "Wondering if I know enough. Always kind of questioning, you know, do I have enough education? So I find myself reading more…ummm…trying to understand things more."

She wonders if she is making the right choices and is concerned about not having all the answers. She gets into a place of negative thinking versus positive thinking and she experiences a personal and internal struggle. She says, "It's an internal struggle for myself. And people might not think that of me. I come off quite competent and knowing and experienced (on the outside) and…and…but inside what's going on is all that self-doubt of, 'Omigosh can I do this?' Like that's my, you know, this is…you only see half of me, the outer me."

Penny especially feels self-doubt when she is out of her comfort zone and is challenged with something new. This is a time when she does not feel grounded. She feels unsure of herself and does not know if she is right or performing her duties in the right way. Self-doubt challenges her self-esteem and her competence. Self-doubt can have different speaking voices too. When she is overwhelmed her voice is squeaky and high pitched. When she is afraid her voice is small, scared and shaky, and when she needs to think things through her voice is loud, clear, and confident.

Penny only lets people see one half of her, which is the half that is the outer, more confident part of herself. The other half is hidden on the inside and this is her self-doubt. This is the place where she does not feel competent, smart, or good enough. However, she is learning how to be more congruent, allowing her inner feelings of self-doubt to show just as equally as her outer presentation of confidence. She recognizes that this process will continue over her lifetime as she strives to live with all the parts of herself more wholistically.

She says, "It (self-doubt) would be in the hidden part, because that's where the uncomfortableness is. I am a confident person and I always have been to some extent and I think over the years with more training and just being more assertive and knowing what I believe in and understanding…being…separating myself from others etcetera. But I think that the self-doubt that I try to hide is in my other half that no-one is supposed to see. But I also find that I don't hide things as much anymore, because, that was hard to do and…ummm…I was even thinking about that the other day, and this is getting a little off the topic of self-doubt, but it still does connect to self-doubt…the split that I have…the dichotomy is that I had a…I used to be so angry as a child and that's…and I think all the way through…a little bit through school too until I started to learn things about myself. But that is what drove me was that anger to prove that I wasn't dumb. I was smart. And so…and I thought, you know, I don't have that anger drive anymore, and I am more integrated, so that…that…you only see the half of me has become more integrated. For example, I want to teach yet I'm so afraid to talk in groups of people…umm… yah…I guess that's still a split. But it's more integrated. I can say, 'Ooooh, this scares me and it's still okay'. Before I used to put on a front and say, 'I'm not affected by this', but that's more of covering up the feelings and thoughts so that no one knows my inadequacies, but now it's like, 'Well, that's how I am!'…more accepting of myself. I'm still an okay person. I can accept both sides of me. I think it will be an ongoing thing for me."

Themes of Self-Doubt

Common themes emerged from the interviews and these were condensed into central themes. The participants share all the central themes (experiences and descriptions of self-doubt, effects of self-doubt, coping with self-doubt, and origins of self-doubt). The table 4.1 on page 80 shows how the participants share many of the common themes.

Table 4.1 Central and Common Themes that Emerged from the Interview Data

Central Themes	Common Themes	Caroline	Marcie	Tracy	Penny
1. Experiences and Descriptions of Self-Doubt	Second guessing self (questioning self)	✓	✓		✓
	Expectations of self and others (measuring up)	✓	✓		✓
	Feeling valued in her work	✓			
	Pressures of the job		✓		
	Confidence on the job			✓	✓
	Lack of clear expectations of a job description			✓	
	Comparing self to others				✓
	Drawings of self-doubt	✓			
	Sand-tray illustration		✓		
	Metaphor examples of self-doubt			✓	✓
	Doing it right (doing the right thing)	✓	✓		
	Positive self-doubt (best practice)	✓	✓	✓	✓
	Negative self-doubt			✓	✓
	Fear of rejection		✓		
	Doing a good enough job		✓	✓	
	Unsure of self		✓		
	Not knowing			✓	✓
	Low self-esteem				✓
2. Effects of Self-Doubt	Bodily reactions	✓	✓	✓	✓
	Pleasing others (being liked)	✓	✓	✓	✓
	Inner dialogue	✓	✓	✓	✓
3. Coping with Self-Doubt	Taking risks	✓	✓	✓	✓
	Being self-aware	✓	✓	✓	✓
	Talking to others	✓		✓	✓
	Having inner resources				✓
	Taking care of self	✓	✓		
	Reflecting on practice		✓		
	Being proactive and positive		✓		
	Having clear boundaries			✓	
	Having a sense of humour			✓	
	Having faith			✓	
	Having trust			✓	
4. Origins of Self-Doubt	Childhood influences		✓	✓	
	Being a hero/perfect			✓	

Discoveries and Impressions

The order in which I present the stories and descriptions is exactly the same order that I interviewed each participant. Caroline was the first person to contact me about being involved in the study, Marcie second, Tracy third, and Penny fourth. I decided to interview them in this same order and then present the findings this way as well. In doing this I established a structure and organization for my study. Moreover, as I read through each story and description presented here, I notice a progression of meaning because I gain a deeper understanding of what self-doubt is and how it is experienced. While each participant's story and description is unique, each experience builds on the others, providing rich and varied descriptions about what self-doubt is and how it impacts practice. This is the value of phenomenological interviewing; magnifying the meaning of the participants' experiences so that a deeper understanding is achieved.

Essence of self-doubt.

Self-doubt is a multifaceted and complex phenomenon that can mean different things to different people, yet at the same time can exhibit commonalities. The rich and varied stories and descriptions can attest to the intricacies and personal meanings self-doubt holds for each participant. Yet as I read through these stories and descriptions I can hear common themes.

As demonstrated in Table 4.1, all participants described self-doubt as involving worry about needing to "measure up" to expectations of self and others. Three out of the four participants described self-doubt as second-guessing or questioning self. Two out of the four stated that self-doubt is about being unsure of self, worrying about "doing it right", achieving confidence on the job, wondering if they are doing a "good enough job", experiencing a negative quality of self-doubt, and simply not knowing. Individual descriptions of self-doubt included a cognitive environment of lack of clear expectations, ambiguous job description, wanting to feel valued, comparing self with others, experiencing pressures of the job, and having low self-esteem.

These essential features of self-doubt suggest that at its core is a *cognitive* component of questioning self. For example, "Am I good enough?" or "Have I done *it* the *right* way?" are typical questions. In addition, there are also *emotive* aspects of self-doubt that can create feelings of uncertainty, worry, fear and anxiety, and *physical* and bodily sensations such as rapid breathing, upset stomach, crying spells, and stiff joints. *Behavioral* aspects include sleepless nights, sulking, poor decision-making, self-reflection, and new learning.

Many described the importance of "paying attention," and "tuning in" to these cues taken from their body, mind, and emotions to learn new ways of responding to this phenomenon while performing on the job. The process of understanding their self-doubt helps these practitioners alter the way they practice so that they begin to respond in healthier and proactive ways. Ultimately how we respond to our experiences of self-doubt can alter how we choose to function in our daily work.

Furthermore, all participants illustrated self-doubt in a creative way either by using metaphors or drawing pictures. This suggests that these participants found it helpful to utilize art and symbols to illustrate what self-doubt means intimately for each of them. Self-doubt *is* a personal journey and in the expression of art and symbol each person was able to give voice to her experience.

Origins of self-doubt.

While all of the participants mentioned childhood influences during the interviews, two of the four discussed this in more detail. For example, Marcie said, "Over my lifetime what I'm realizing more and more is that there are events that happen in the present that are tripping me back to the past. I think as a child growing up I had a real emphasis on being an "example" (to be a good girl and to meet other people's expectations). Penny said, "Well, I think it goes way back. Like I think I'm really little. I . . . I . . . I think I just always expected a lot out of myself. I think I was born into my family to make them happy. I think it was always part of just wanting to be good at whatever I did and then, but always doubting my ability in whatever I did, and I think that carries into my work today." According to Langford and Clance (1993), Clance (1985), Clance and O'Toole (1987), and Clance and Imes (1978) messages from families of origin and childhood can have an effect on the development of self and the imposter phenomenon. The cited examples above suggest that this is true for self-doubt as well. It would be fascinating to explore the relationship between childhood and the development of self, self-doubt, and the imposter phenomenon in more depth.

Categories of self-doubt.

The participants all spoke of self-doubt as being either negative or positive. Negative self-doubt is described as debilitating, overwhelming, nauseating, and compelling. The descriptions of self-doubt are rich with metaphors of being lost, feeling stuck, landing in quicksand, being in a fog, not seeing the light, expecting the worst, imagining "catastrophes", making "mountains out of mole-hills", and seeing only "half of the self". Even though these descriptions are very different they share a common quality of distress.

Positive self-doubt is described as a way of learning about self and of remaining healthy in the field. It becomes a positive force when it helps practitioners to reflect critically on their practice so that they can perform more competently. As the four participants experienced their self-doubt and learned from it, they became more introspective and self-reflective about how to function in practice. All the participants spoke of moving beyond the doubt and acknowledging the significant lessons learned when they became overwhelmed by their negative self-doubt. For example, early in practice the experience of self-doubt was devastating for the participants, yet all talked about how they turned this around in their practice. This is critical for avoiding burnout and fostering resiliency. Caroline spoke of getting stronger within herself. When her inner strengths and outer expectations are equal and parallel then she is able to see more light and opportunities in her work because she values herself more. Marcie spoke of needing to balance her negative experiences with positive inner dialogue to discover what her triggers can teach her about herself. She finds this process helpful to go beyond the doubt rather than staying stuck in it. Tracy recognizes that taking a more positive attitude toward self-doubt helps her to take a more active role in her practice to do things differently and create an approach of "best practice". She says she definitely does not like being in the quicksand too long!! Penny acknowledges the importance of learning from her mistakes and naming the self-doubt so that she can start to give herself more positive affirmations. She also spoke about it being important to "not hide" parts of the self, but to strive for congruency and balance. Being congruent and self-aware in practice means bringing the inner and the outer parts of the self together so that practitioners can "walk their talk" and "talk their walk" (do what they say and say what they do) and feel more confident in their capabilities and more satisfied in their work.

  Seeking creativity and making mistakes is significant in helping practitioners discover the lessons they need to learn in their practice to create feelings of hope rather than debilitating feelings of self-doubt. For example, Caroline spoke of the light bulb, in her last drawing (figure 4.4) helping her to see better when she is in the fog of self-doubt. She says, "Well, in the fog things don't look as bright. The world just doesn't have the same kind of shine or sparkle. And then as the . . . as the self-doubt gets smaller (the fog), the light bulb appears to be bigger. The light bulb is always there . . . it's just a matter of whether I *see* that it's there and whether I *believe* that I can reach out to that idea." Marcie stated, "And there will be more lessons to learn and the self-doubt is just saying, even if I lose my balance I'm moving forward. So the self-doubt are my fears and my fears, well, I'd have to say they're my friends too. They have sparked me to do things differently and it's like dancing with the dark side to see more light."

Management of self-doubt.

The movement from negative to positive self-doubt, as illustrated above, indicates that a keen awareness of self is needed to begin to learn how to manage and cope effectively. Being self-aware, talking to others, and taking care of self are the three most popular techniques which these participants used. As indicated in table 4.1 other individual coping skills are described such as taking risks, having a sense of humour, and maintaining clear boundaries.

Talking about self-doubt with others in a supportive and trusting work environment is essential for practitioners to achieve resiliency and sustainability in their work. Sharing experiences of self-doubt with others lessens the impact of the overwhelming nature that can fuel the negative quality of self-doubt. Looking within and sharing personal and intimate experiences with others, who are trustworthy, supportive, and non-judgmental, can help practitioners to process the role their self-doubt plays out in their practice. Much meaning and understanding is gained. Penny stated she becomes more grounded and gains more clarity in her work after talking things through with someone who truly listens to her in a non-judgmental way. She says, "I had to talk about it. I had to talk about what was going on for me with someone and when I did, I could reflect on it and learn from the experience because I did not feel judged by that person". Marcie also stated she learns from talking about her self-doubt with others and that this learning is life long.

Further, staying alert to self-doubt in practice brings a humbleness to the work and helps in the understanding of the complexities of life with which the clients are struggling. During her interview Penny state, "There needs to be some healthy self-doubt in there to keep me humble". A time for humility, for self-examination, and for openly acknowledging doubt creates awareness, which facilitates change in the practitioner so that arrogance is avoided and learning is enhanced. It is important that practitioners and their supervisors engage in a dialogue about feelings of self-doubt and how they impact practice. Tracy stated, "Yeah, there needs to be some outside feedback, some mirror that says, 'Yeah, you're okay, you're cool, do your thing.' I had the best supervisor of my life who taught me lots about myself and my self-doubts!" Also when Tracy is in the quicksand of self doubt she says she needs someone to help her out, as she indicates, "The more I fight it (self-doubt) the more I sink and I need somebody to throw me a rope (to listen)."

In addition, self-care is another coping skill which the participants used to manage their self-doubt and maintain a balanced and healthy professional life. For example, Caroline spoke of wanting a balance between self-doubt and self-care to help her feel good about the job she is doing. Marcie talked about nurturing herself by being in tune with all aspects and layers (the sunshine and self-doubt parts) of herself so that she can operate from a more authentic place. When Tracy sets clear boundaries, relies on her faith, and trusts her sense of humour, she maintains a healthy and positive attitude towards her self-doubt. Penny uses self-care techniques, such as reading, reflecting, affirming herself, getting enough sleep, and changing her thinking to help her understand her self and self-doubt better. Thus, child and youth care educators and clinical supervisors could include a specific piece about self-reflection in their courses or supervision sessions to address practitioner self-care with an emphasis on self-doubt in practice.

Summary.

Self-doubt informs and shapes professional practice. Knowing and understanding self-doubt in relation to working with children, youth, and families is necessary for maintaining healthy boundaries and developing interventions that support the client's needs. Exploring self-doubt in practice helps practitioners accept all aspects of themselves, negative and positive, to enhance their growth and to seek more clarity in their work. For example, Caroline has learned that it is important to become more aware of her own boundaries, values, and beliefs about her work and how these affect how she experiences self-doubt in her practice. Marcie notes self-doubt expands her knowledge of who she is and what she does in her work as a child and youth care practitioner. Tracy speaks about double-checking procedures in her practice and exploring ways of "crossing her Is and Ts" as this could impact a child or youth's care. Penny believes that working on her inner (self-doubt) self and outer (confident) self brings more understanding of who she is and what she does in her work. Given these experiences, child and youth care educators and clinical supervisors could provide more opportunities for students and professionals to explore their self-doubt and how it impacts their practice.

Discussing and revealing the innermost thoughts, emotions, and bodily sensations of self-doubt help child and youth care practitioners to examine and identify who they are and what they do in their practice. Sharing stories with each other helps professionals know that they are not alone and that looking within helps them to be and work to their fullest capacity. Self-doubt is a healthy and beneficial part of the journey towards establishing an effective and resilient practice. Once the light bulb comes on and awareness is heightened, self-doubt meets self-assurance and practitioners can function better. There is more confidence, congruency, and balance in practice. Exploring, describing, and analyzing self-doubt can indeed be a powerful self-awareness tool!

CHAPTER FIVE
Finale

There are four primary functions of scholarly inquiry...
1. personal transformation
2. the improvement of professional practice
3. the generation of knowledge
4. appreciation of the complexity, intricacy, structure and –
some would say – beauty of reality.

Valerie Malhotra Bentz & Jeremy Shapiro   (1998, p.68)

Implications for Child and Youth Care Practice

This research has provided some insight into what it is like to experience self-doubt in child and youth care practice and may assist us in the development of a greater appreciation and understanding of the inner world of the professional. The findings presented here can help practitioners to practice in more meaningful and purposeful ways by helping them to examine their self-doubt more closely. Krueger (1991) points out that being a child and youth care practitioner is about "… caring and acting – about being there, thinking on your feet, interacting, and growing with children" (p.77). When practitioners gain an understanding of their self-doubt they have the opportunity to establish emotional stability and face their clients' often distressing experiences, because they have worked through some of their own. Talking to others and sharing doubts brings more passion and commitment to the work. Krueger (1991) notes further that "…with the help of supervisors, teammates, and teachers [child and youth care practitioners] have to constantly strive to understand their own feelings and experiences in relationship to [know] how they influence interactions with children and families" (p. 82).

The awareness of self is essential for understanding child and youth care work as noted by Fewster (1990, 1999), Krueger (1997), Rose (1991), Kass and Mann-Feder (1995), and Ricks (1989). An understanding of self-doubt encourages further exploration and awareness of self in practice. This exploration leads to new knowledge about who one is, what one does, and how one does *it* in child and youth care. When children, youth, and families are in the care of professionals it is vital for the professionals to feel competent and responsible in their practice. Ricks (1989) indicates:

> In order for learners to examine, understand, and integrate self they need knowledge about self and how it works; they need skills in reflecting and changing self; and they need to integrate this knowledge and these skills in their child and youth care practice. Once the knowledge about self and how it works and the skills of reflecting on and changing self are integrated into one's daily child and youth care practice, one can be responsible and accountable for one's child care practice. (p. 3)

Thus exploring self-doubt in one's practice helps the practitioner to recognize strengths, learn from mistakes, gain more confidence, and above all, to examine self in order to gain a deeper understanding of experiences and interactions in professional practice.

Further Research

While this study has helped with a first step to understanding what four child and youth care practitioners experience when they experience self-doubt in their practice, future studies could take the inquiry further. For example, utilizing the "Maslach Burnout Inventory" (Maslach, 1982) and the "Imposter Phenomenon Scale" (Clance, 1985) to discover relationships between self-doubt, burnout, and the imposter phenomenon could inform the field about the reasons why child and youth care practitioners experience burnout. What percentage of child and youth care practitioners who experience burnout experience self-doubt? Do they also experience characteristics of the imposter phenomenon? Can the presence of self-doubt predict burnout? Also Oleson, Poehlmann, Yost, Lynch, and Arkin (2000) developed a "Subjective Overachievement Scale" and this tool could be used to measure the presence of self-doubt and to discover what percentage of child and youth care practitioners experience self-doubt in their practice – daily, weekly, monthly, seldom, never.

Moreover, as noted earlier, a limitation to this inquiry is a lack of male representation. Further research could explore the relationship between gender and self-doubt. Are there gender implications and if so what are they? Do males experience self-doubt differently than females? A recent study, Evans, Bryant, Owens, and Koukos (2004) explored ethnic differences in burnout, coping strategies, and attitudes toward stress management interventions in childcare professionals. Interestingly, in this study the participants were all female childcare professionals. They found that ethnicity was predictive of some aspects of burnout (emotional exhaustion and depersonalization) and that coping strategies play a stronger role in the development and maintenance of burnout. They note interventions aimed at encouraging the sharing of one's frustrations and the telling of one's story, as well as, the teaching of stress management techniques, journal writing strategies, and relaxation methods will benefit childcare professionals and the quality of care provided.

Another area for further research could involve looking at child and youth care curricula. How do educational programs provide child and youth care students with enough opportunities to explore their self-doubts, as well as their competencies, in practice? Do they incorporate stress management techniques, journal writing strategies, and other self-care methods into their curricula? The authors, Corey and Corey (2003), of a common text used in child and youth care curricula, share personal feelings of their doubts openly and encourage students to face their own feelings of incompetence and self-doubt, as well as competence in practice. They also include chapters on stress and burnout, and self-care. Training programs need to create a safe environment where students can explore feelings of self-doubt and question their competence so that they may develop the skills needed to reflect critically on their practice. Students also need opportunities to explore self-care techniques to maintain their resilience.

Even though I have come to the end of my study, there seems to be a natural movement of asking more questions. Research does not end with one study it merely offers inspiration and an invitation to continue the journey.

Conclusion

This inquiry has listened to the voice of self-doubt of four child and youth care practitioners and has generated new knowledge and understanding regarding this phenomenon. The rationale for designing and implementing this study grew from my own personal experiences of self-doubt and a curiosity of what others experience. Professionals can learn and understand much about themselves when they look into their own world, as well as the world of others, and they can learn about and understand their world, and another's, by looking into themselves.

This research has explained what four participants experienced when they experienced self-doubt in their child and youth care practice. It has described what self-doubt looks like and feels like for these people, illustrated how self-doubt affects their practice, and demonstrated what these practitioners have learned from their experiences. Sharing the stories and descriptions triggered insight and a response in each participant and helped her to create change and action in her own professional life. Such research gives the opportunity of discovering knowledge that is liberating and as Palys (1997) states:

> In this regard, one of the major contributions [I] can make in [my] research is merely to open [our] eyes and recognize the strength inherent in the diversity that already exists. By changing how we *think* about ourselves and about each other, we change who we are and who we can be. (p. 400)

It is important to continue to listen to the self-doubt voice and to dialogue with others in order to promote the growth and development of the child and youth care professional.

References

Abel, E. K. & Nelson, M. K. (1990). Circles of care: An introductory essay. In E. K.Abel and M. K. Nelson (Eds.), *Circles of care: Work and identity in women's lives.* Albany, NY: State University of New York Press.

Abrams, L. J. & Kessler, S. (2002). The inner world of the genetic counselor. *Journal of Genetic Counseling, 11(1),* 5-17.

Allen, T. N. (1997). *The "imposter phenomenon" in graduate counseling students and practicing school counsellors.* Unpublished master's thesis, University of Victoria, Victoria, British Columbia, Canada.

Bandura, A. & Adams, N. (1977). Analysis of self-efficacy theory of behavioral change. *Cognitive Therapy and Research, 1(4)*, 287-310.

Bandura, A. (1980). Gauging the relationship between self-efficacy judgments and actions. *Cognitive Therapy and Research, 4(2),* 263-268.

Bandura, A. (1989). Human agency in social cognitive theory. *American Psychologist, 44 (9)*, 1175-1184.

Bandura, A (1997). *Self-efficacy: The exercise of control.* New York, NY: W. H. Freeman and Company.

Belenky, M., Clinchy, B., Goldberger, N., & Tarule, J. (1986). *Women's ways of knowing: The development of self, voice, and mind.* New York: Basic Books.

Bendixen, L. D. (2002). A process model of epistemic belief change. In B. K. Hofer & P.R. Pintrich (Eds.), *Personal epistemology: The psychology of beliefs about knowledge and knowing.* Mahwah, NJ: Lawrence Erlbaum Associates.

Bentz, V. M. & Shapiro, J. J. (1998). *Mindful inquiry in social research.* Thousand Oaks, CA: Sage.

Boeree, G. C. (1998). *Qualitative methods workbook.* Retrieved February 14, 2002, from http://www.ship.edu/cgboeree/qual/meth.html

Boyd, B. J. & Pasley, B. K. (1989). Role stress as a contributor to burnout in child care professionals. *Child and Youth Care Quarterly, 18(4),* 243-258.

Brookfield, S. (1994). Tales from the dark side: A phenomenography of adult critical reflection. *International Journal of Lifelong Learning Education, 13 (3),* 203-216.

Clance, P. R. & Imes, S. A. (1978). The imposter phenomenon in high achieving women: Dynamics and therapeutic intervention. *Psychotherapy: Theory, Research and Practice, 15 (3)*, 241-247.

Clance, P. R. (1985). *The imposter phenomenon: Overcoming the fear that haunts your success.* Atlanta, GA: Peachtree.

Clance, P. R. & O'Toole, M. A. (1987). The imposter phenomenon: An internal barrier to empowerment and achievement. *Women – and – Therapy, 6 (3)*, 51-64.

Colaizzi, P. (1973). *Reflection and research in psychology.* Dubuque: Kendall-Hunt.

Colaizzi, P. (1978). Psychological research as a phenomenologist views it. In R. Valle& M. King (Eds.), *Existential-phenomenological alternatives for psychology.* New York, NY: Oxford University Press.

Corey, M. S. & Corey, C. (2003). *Becoming a helper (4th ed.).* Pacific Grove, CA: Brooks/Cole.

Creswell, J.W. (1998). *Qualitative inquiry and research design choosing among five traditions.* Thousand Oaks, CA: Sage.

Denzin, N. K. (1989). *The research act: A theoretical introduction to sociological methods (3rd. ed.).* Eaglewood Cliffs, NJ: Prentice Hall.

Eckroth-Bucher, M. (2001). Philosophical basis and practice of self-awareness in psychiatric nursing. *Journal of Psychosocial Nursing and Mental Health Services, 39 (2),* 32-39.

Ehrlich, F.M. (2001). Levels of self-awareness: Countertransference in psychoanalysis, couple, and family therapy. *Contemporary Psychoanalysis, 37(2),* 283-296.

Elks, M. A. & Kirkhart, K. E. (1993). Evaluating effectiveness from the practitioner perspective. *Social Work, 38 (5),* 554-563.

Ely, M., Vinz, R., Downing, M. & Anzul, M. (1997). *On writing qualitative research: living by words.* London, UK: The Falmer Press.

Evans, G. D., Bryant, N. E., Owens, J. S. & Koukos, K. (2004). Ethnic differences in burnout, coping, and intervention acceptability among childcare professionals. *Child & Youth Care Forum, 33 (5),* 349-371.

Fewster, G. (1990). *Being in child care: A journey into self.* New York, NY: Haworth Press.

Fewster, G. (1999). Turning my self inside out: My theory of me. *Journal of Child and Youth Care, 13(2),* 35-54.

Freudenberger, H. J. (1977). Burn-out: Occupational hazard of the child care worker. *Child Care Quarterly, 6 (2),* 90-99.

Gall, M. D., Borg, W. R. & Gall, J. P. (1996). *Educational research: An introduction (6th ed.).* New York, NY: Longman.

Gendler, J. R. (1984, 1988). *The book of qualities.* New York, NY: Harper Perennial.

Gerson, B. (1996). Introduction. In B. Gerson (Ed.), *The therapist as a person: Life crises, life choices, life experiences, and their effects on treatment.* Hillsdale, NJ: The Analytic Press.

Giorgi, A. (1975). An application of phenomenological method. In A. Giorgi, C. Fischer, & E. Murphy (Eds.), *Duquesne studies in phenomenological psychology (Vol.II).* Pittsburgh, PA: Duquesne University Press.

Giorgi, A. (1985). Sketch of a psychological phenomenological method. In A. Giorgi (Ed.), *Phenomenology and psychological research.* Pittsburgh, P.A: Duquesne University Press.

Goelman, H. & Guo, H. (1998). What we know and what we don't know about burnout among early childhood care providers. *Child & Youth Care Forum, 27 (3),*175-199.

Goldberg, C. (1988). The life cycle of the practitioner. *Psychotherapy in Private Practice, 5(4),*15-26.

Goldberg, C. (1993). The unexplored in self-analysis. *Psychotherapy, 30 (1),* 159-161.

Hathaway, E. H. (1999). *Psyche's virtual reality: A psychological exploration of self-doubt in the experience and structure of the post-modern self.* Dissertation Abstracts International, 61 (9-B), 4984 (UMI No. 9987392).

Hermann, A. D., Leonardelli, G. J. & Arkin, R. M. (2002). Self-doubt and self-esteem: A threat from within. *Personality and Social Psychology Bulletin, 28 (3),* 395-408.

Hiebert, B., Uhlemann, M., Marshall, A. & Lee, D. Y. (1998). The relationship between self-talk, anxiety, and counselling skill. *Canadian Journal of Counselling, 32 (2),* 163-171.

Hycner, R. H. (1985). Some guidelines for the phenomenological analysis of interview data. *Human Studies, 8,* 279-303.

Janesick, V. J. (1994). The dance of qualitative research design: Metaphor, methodolarty, and meaning. In N. K. Denzin & Y. J. Lincoln (Eds.). *Handbook of qualitative research.* Thousand Oaks, CA: Sage.

Junge, M. B. & Linesch, D. (1993). Our own voices: New paradigms for art therapy research. *The Arts in Psychotherapy, 20 (1),* 61-67.

Kass, R. & Mann-Feder, V. (1995). Identifyimg helping preferences: A workshop model for stimulating self-reflection in child and youth care workers. *Journal of Child and Youth Care, 10 (3),* 37-42.

Keen, E. (1975). *A primer in phenomenological psychology.* New York, NY: Holt, Reinhart and Winston, Inc.

Krueger, M. (1991). Coming from your center, being there, teaming up, meeting them where they're at, interacting together, counseling on the go, creating circles of care, discovering and using self, and caring for one another: Central themes in professional child and youth care. *Journal of Child and Youth Care, 5 (1),* 77-87.

Krueger, M. (1997). Using self, story, and intuition to understand child and youth care work. *Child and Youth Care Forum, 26(3),* 153-161.

Kvale, S. (1996). *Interviews: An introduction to qualitative research interviewing.* Thousand Oaks, CA: Sage.

Lambert, B. (1994). Beating burnout: A multi-dimensional perspective. *AECA Resource Book Series, 1 (2).* Watson, Australia: Australian Early Childhood Association.

Langford, J. & Clance, P. R. (1993). The imposter phenomenon: Recent research findings regarding dynamic, personality and family patterns and their implications for treatment. *Psychotherapy, 30 (3),* 495-501.

Lauterbach, S. S. & Becker, P. H. (1996). Caring for self: Becoming a self-reflective nurse. *Holistic Nursing Practice, 10 (2),* 57-68.

Maisel, E. (1996). *Affirmations for artists.* New York, NY: Tarcher/Putnam.

Manlove, E. (1993). Multiple correlates of burnout in child care workers. *Early Childhood Research Quarterly, 8,* 499-518.

Marshall, C. & Rossman, G. B. (1999). *Designing qualitative research (3rd ed.)* Thousand Oaks, CA: SAGE.

Maslach, C. (1982). *Burnout: The cost of caring.* Englewood Cliffs, NJ: Prentice-Hall.

Maslach, C.M. & Pines, A. (1977). The burn-out syndrome in the day care setting. *Child Care Quarterly, 6(2),* 100-114.

Mattingly, M. A. (1977). Sources of stress and burnout in professional child care work. *Child Care Quarterly, 6 (2),* 127-137.

May, R. (1989). *The art of counseling (revised edition).* New York, NY: Gardner Press.

McMullen, M. B. & Krantz, M. (1988). Burnout in day care workers: The effects of learned helplessness and self-esteem. *Child & Youth Care Quarterly, 17 (4),*275-280.

McNiff, S. (1996). Freedom of research and artistic inquiry. *The Arts in Psychotherapy, 13 (4),* 279-284.

Meloy, J. M. (1994). *Writing the qualitative dissertation: Understanding by doing.* Hillsdale, N.J: Lawrence Erlbaum.

Mezirow, J. (1990). How critical reflection triggers transformative learning. In J. Mezirow and Associates (Eds.), *Fostering critical reflection in adulthood.* San Francisco, CA: Jossey-Bass.

Moustakas, C. (1967). *Creativity and conformity.* New York, NY: Van Nostrand Reinhold.

Moustakas, C. (1994). *Phenomenological research methods.* Thousand Oaks, CA: Sage.

Neuman, W. L. (2004). *Basics of social research: Qualitative and quantitative approaches.* Boston, MA: Allyn and Bacon.

Oleson, K. C., Poehlmann, K. M., Yost, J. H., Lynch, M. E. & Arkin, R. M. (2000). Subjective overachievement: Individual differences in self-doubt and concern with performance. *Journal of Personality, 68 (3),* 491-524.

Palys, T. (1997). *Research decisions: Quantitative and qualitative perspectives (2nd ed.).* Toronto, ON: Harcourt Brace.

Parry, P. (1989). The influence of women in child and youth care. *Journal of Child and Youth Care Work, 5,* 17-25.

Parry, P. (1992). Do I see what you see? Gender sensitivities in child and youth care practice. *Journal of Child and Youth Care, 7(2),* 11-20.

Paul, L. J. (1999). Phenomenology as a method for the study of informal care, *Journal-of-Family-Studies, 5 (2),* 192-206.

Pelham, B. W. (1991). On confidence and consequence: The certainty and importance of self-knowledge. *Journal of Personality and Social Psychology, 60 (4),* 518-530.

Pines, A. & Aronson, E. (1998). *Career burnout: Causes and curses.* New York, NY: The Free Press.

Pollio, H. R., Henley, T. & Thompson, C. B. (1997). *The phenomenology of everyday life.* Cambridge, U.K.: Cambridge University Press.

Polkinghorne, D. E. (1989). Phenomenological research methods. In R. S. Valle & S. Halling (Eds.), *Existential-phenomenological perspectives in psychology.* New York, NY: Plenum Press.

Portnow, K. E. (1996). *Dialogues of doubt: The psychology of self-doubt and emotional gaslighting in adult women and men.* Dissertation Abstracts International, 57(7-B), 4750 (UMI No. 9638768).

Ray, M. A. (1994). The richness of phenomenology: Philosophic, theoretic, and methodologic concerns. In J. M. Morse (Ed.), *Critical issues in qualitative research methods.* Thousand Oaks, CA: SAGE.

Ricks, F. (1989). Self-awareness model for training and application in child and youth care. *Journal of Child and Youth Care, 4 (1),* 33-41.

Ricks, F. (1992). A feminist's view of caring. *Journal of Child and Youth Care, 7(2)*, 49-57.

Resta, R. (2002). Commentary on the inner world of the genetic counselor: The unexamined counseling life. *Journal of Genetic Counseling, 11(1)*, 19-22.

Rogers, C. (1961). *On becoming a person.* Boston, MA: Houghton Mifflin Co., Sentry Edition.

Rose, L. (1991). On being a child and youth care worker. *Journal of Child and Youth Care, 5 (1)*, 21-26.

Rousseve, R.J. (1969). Counselor, know thyself!: Inquest of a viable model of the human condition as a perspective for professional effectiveness. *Personnel and Guidance Journal, 47(7)*, 628-633.

Rubin, H.J. & Rubin, I.S. (1995). *Qualitative interviewing: The art of hearing data.* Thousand Oaks, CA: Sage.

Savicki, V. (1993). Clarification of child and youth care identity through an analysis of work environment and burnout. *Child and Youth Care Forum, 22 (6)*, 441-457.

Schön, D. A. (1983). *The reflective practitioner: How professionals think in action.* New York, NY: Basic Books

Seidman, I. E. (1991). *Interviewing as qualitative research: A guide for researchers in education and the social sciences.* New York, NY: Teachers College Press.

Sladde, L. R. (2001). Where are the women? *CYC Online, 32.* Retrieved April 26, 2004 from http://www.cyc-net.org/cyc-online/cycol-0901-sladde.html.

Sokolowski, R. (2000). *Introduction to phenomenology.* Cambridge, UK: Cambridge University Press.

Tesch, R. (1980). *Phenomenological and transformative research: What they are and how to do them.* Santa Barbara: Fielding occasional papers.

van Manen, M. (1997). *Researching lived experience (2nd ed.).* London, ON, Canada: The Althouse Press.

Wimett, L. C. (1992). *Perceived self-efficiency of medical/surgical registered nurses.* Unpublished doctoral dissertation, University of Missouri, Columbia.

Appendices

Appendix A: Flyer
Appendix B: Interview Questions
Appendix C: Photography of Art Release and Consent Form
Appendix D: Confidentiality Agreement for Typist/Transcriber

Appendix A
FLYER

Date: _____

ARE YOU INTERESTED IN EXPLORING SELF-DOUBT IN YOUR PRACTICE?

If you answered **yes** to this question and are a child and youth care practitioner, would you be willing to describe your experiences as a part of a research project? As a participant, you will be asked to describe your experiences of self-doubt in one 120-minute audio-taped interview, one 60-minute audio-taped interview, and participate in one 60-minute follow-up meeting. Interviews will be confidential. Participation is voluntary and participants may end their involvement at any time.

IT CAN BE A VERY REWARDING EXPERIENCE!

The exploration of pertinent personal and professional experiences through self-reflection can be a meaningful and helpful exercise. Telling your story about self-doubt may help you to clarify your own thoughts and give you a deeper understanding of yourself as an authentic practitioner. This process may also inspire others to look at their own experience in practice as well.

PLEASE CONTACT: Heather Sanrud   **BY: August 31, 2003**

Appendix B

INTERVIEW QUESTIONS

What do you experience when you experience self-doubt in your practice?

What does self-doubt look like?

How does self-doubt affect your practice?

What does it mean when you doubt yourself in practice?

What do you feel when you experience self-doubt in practice?

When do you experience these feelings of self-doubt?

What do you do when you experience self-doubt in practice?

What are you doubting when you doubt self?

What different kinds of self-doubt have you experienced?

How do you know you are experiencing self-doubt in your practice?

What have you learned from your experiences of self-doubt?

Appendix C
PHOTOGRAPHY OF ART RELEASE & CONSENT FORM

I_____, hereby authorize
        (participant's name)

_____, to photograph art work done
        (researcher's name)

by me, during the period from_____ to _____,
with the understanding that (please check boxes):

[ ]   My real name/identity will not be disclosed.
[ ]   This is for educational purpose to aid in research.
[ ]   Some details of my experience may be included, while protecting my identity.
[ ]   This photograph may be included in the body of the work.

Any further comments, restrictions or authorization (the participant may provide information in the space provided below):

Signed: _____   Witnessed: _____
Date: _____   Date: _____

Appendix D

CONFIDENTIALITY AGREEMENT FOR TYPIST/TRANSCRIBER

I _____ agree to protect the anonymity

(typist/transcriber)

and confidentiality of the participants while typing or transcribing

any data produced for the research project entitled, *Listening to the Self-*

Doubt Voice: What do Child and Youth Care Practitioners Experience?

I understand that each participant will be given a pseudonym.

Signed: _____

Witnessed: _____

Date: _____

i want morebooks!

Buy your books fast and straightforward online - at one of world's fastest growing online book stores! Environmentally sound due to Print-on-Demand technologies.

Buy your books online at
www.get-morebooks.com

Kaufen Sie Ihre Bücher schnell und unkompliziert online – auf einer der am schnellsten wachsenden Buchhandelsplattformen weltweit! Dank Print-On-Demand umwelt- und ressourcenschonend produziert.

Bücher schneller online kaufen
www.morebooks.de

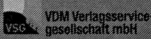 VDM Verlagsservicegesellschaft mbH
Heinrich-Böcking-Str. 6-8   Telefon: +49 681 3720 174   info@vdm-vsg.de
D - 66121 Saarbrücken   Telefax: +49 681 3720 1749   www.vdm-vsg.de

Printed by
Schaltungsdienst Lange o.H.G., Berlin